The 9 Mirages of Love

How to Stop Chasing What Doesn't Exist

Chiara Mazzucco

This book is dedicated to the baby boy growing inside me. Luca, may you grow up to know your worth and treat love kindly.

Don't be a dick.

And to my husband for being everything I never knew existed. Thank you for always being my strength.

Acknowledgements

My friends. For always coming to me and trusting my advice. You've taught me everything there is to know about love and I don't know where I would be without you today. Thank you for being my shoulders to cry on and for always believing in me. And thank you for providing me with endless material for my work. I love you. You've made me the luckiest girl alive.

My husband. Without you, I would have never picked up a pen again. You've guided me, believed in me, supported me, and put up with all of my insanities. You are the most amazing man; you are my perfection.

My parents. Because you've taught me what it means to truly be meant for one another. Mom, you bring magic back into my life when reality swallows it whole. Dad, every day you are my inspiration. Thank you for believing in me… I hope I make you proud.

About the Author

Chiara is a tough, reality loving blogger based out of Los Angeles, CA. After dipping her feet in different career waters and repeatedly resurfacing without a pulse, she's nestled safely into the world of writing about sex, dating and relationships.

Photo by: Stephen Albanese

Website: **www.chiarasays.com**
Email: **Chiara@chiarasays.com**
Facebook: **www.facebook.com/chiarasays**
Twitter: @iChiaraSays

Table of Contents

Preface

Love destroyed me when I was younger. It made me a bitter, cynical, bratty little drama queen that no one wanted to be around.

I started ChiaraSays.com because once my friends started falling in and out of love, I stopped wanting to be around *them* anymore, and that wasn't okay. When it comes to love, I can't tolerate bitching and moaning and overdrawn theatrics. So, I started writing articles based on real life dramas affecting their lives, like, for example, how to stop loving someone who doesn't love you back (Appendix B). And I started solving their problems there. As my brutal, raw and uncensored advice poured out, the broken hearts came flooding in.

Every email I received read like the ones before it. And although the specifics varied – i.e. he slept with my sister vs. she slept with my brother – each email was written with the same tone: denial. I started to wonder what the hell it was that made these people so damn stubborn, and how in God's name was I going to fix it? What began as a pastime quickly turned into a full-blown sense of duty. Someone needs to slap you back into reality.

The reason love made me a bitter bitch is because there was no one there to wake me up from my self-induced nightmares. I had pushed everyone so far away that no one was left to tell me I was chasing something that didn't exist. There was no one there to promise me a better tomorrow and no one there to tell me I was worth more than the constant denial flowing through my vulnerable, weakened veins.

That is why, loyal reader, I took on the task of writing *The 9 Mirages of Love - How to Stop Chasing What Doesn't Exist*. I needed each one of these reality slaps at one point in my life, and there was no one there to give them to me. All I wanted was for someone to remind me I was worth the proverbial "it", and that I would get through whatever emotional Armageddon I was experiencing. Lucky for you, I've been there, learned some and am here to help *you*. I'm about to dish you a piping hot plate of reality. Slap.

Please know I am *not* a licensed psychologist, and if reading this book doesn't shift any gears or make you feel any better you need to seek professional help. Having said that, most of the emotional roller coaster you are experiencing is completely natural, and you are not the first one to struggle with it.

I don't believe in sugarcoating anything in life, especially when it comes to love. If you're being an obsessive, clingy and delusional creep, you can bet your ass I will make sure to bring it to your attention and tell you how to stop.

Introduction

Love fucking sucks. You would think we had enough self-help books at our disposal to paint our relationships in picture-perfect colors. Yet, as bright and plentiful as that rainbow-colored section is in the bookstore, we still can't figure out why men marry bitches, why we fall in love with heartbreakers, why men and women come from different planets, and why shows like Jerry Springer still exist.

Life is full of complexities and love is usually to blame. We'd like to believe we're above clichés and that we'll never be caught dead in a self-help isle, but the truth is we are slaves to love and will risk anything to attain it - even if it means pushing everyone away to create our own reality. Stupid love; it makes us justify irrational behavior and turn our backs on the red flags that would otherwise have us running the opposite direction.

Creating your own reality is usually when the shit hits the fan. Love is like a drug addiction; when you're in too deep, you're able to justify every line you snort by freely feeding irrational wishful thinking. But what happens when you're no longer able to come back? When you've pushed everyone away and there is no one left to guide you home?

Why You Bought This Book

Imagine being stranded in the desert. Your body begins to violently experience the first signs of dehydration; you're no longer sweating; your muscles are cramping; you're lightheaded and your heartbeats are becoming irregular. You can't cry because your body saves what little water it has left for organ function. After days of crawling through what seems like a torturous nightmare, you see a pool of water up ahead and waves of hope radiate through your weak veins. You use the little energy you have left and make a sprint for salvation. Only you never find it. This, ladies and gentlemen, is a mirage.

You're probably shaking your head right now, whispering that you've never even been to the desert and this book is not for you. If I were there, this would be the moment I'd slap you across the face. You may not be stranded in a desert, but you are still chasing something that doesn't exist. Whether it'd be perfection, monogamy, or hope for change, we are all guilty of letting our wishful thinking get the best of us.

Unfortunately, distinguishing the difference between reality and wishful thinking is significantly harder to do while deep in the state of love, lust or obsession. The reality is: you're still wishing on a falling star and blowing out birthday candles, hoping for reality and wishful thinking to become one. Just because love is blind doesn't mean reality isn't happening. And, as it continues to happen, once it's all said and done, you're the asshole left with a box of tissues and prearranged therapy sessions to deal with your broken heart. All because you were too hooked on hope and ignored the facts of the situation: you're in a desert and there is no fucking lake surrounded by palm trees with little dancing women passing out blended margaritas. *WAKE UP!*

The first, most important, and hardest step towards recovery is realizing that you have a problem. Now, I'm not trying to slap you with a ton of clichés here, but let's face it: up until now, you've been certain things will take a turn for the better, dancing in candy-land and ignoring all of the red flags. But there's a reason you've picked up this book: deep inside, you know something needs to change. Even if you can't quite put your finger on it, you know you're not in a healthy relationship. Whether it's done consciously or subconsciously, you're finding ways to scream for help.

First and foremost, I'll help you identify the actual mirage you're chasing. You're not crazy, that little tickle in your gut is actually real. For all those times your partner has made you feel like a crazy person for being suspicious or has injected you with a syringe full of unreachable hope, you'll soon be able to see yourself from a different perspective once you see what you're *really* up against.

Secondly, you'll see how common each mirage is. It's easy to believe each romance is unique. And while the details vary from relationship to relationship, certain qualities remain the same. Realizing that others are in similar situations can help you find a way out of the denial you're in. Often times, we don't want to believe a relationship is harmful because we like to cling to the details we assume are unique. *No one knows what we're like behind closed doors! We're soul mates!*

Thirdly, we'll go through characteristics of each mirage and if (that's a BIG if) there are ways to salvage the relationship, I'll provide you with some tips and tricks to get you through it. The advice won't be sugarcoated and I'll probably do everything in my power to keep you from salvaging it; but in the name of the complexities in life, if there's a chance to fix the relationship, I'll give it to you.

And lastly, I don't just hold your hand as you realize you're in a dead-end relationship; I give you a way out. Chapter 13 is a guide to breaking up. If this doesn't work, you can always dish out your hard earned money and sign up for that expensive therapy session you've been dreading. But I've got to warn you, your new expensive therapist will just tell you what I'm telling you... only it'll be in a much nicer, more expensive way.

I've included a few articles – also available on ChiaraSays.com – that I think you'd like to keep handy. I put them in the back for your convenience.

A Book To Keep On the Shelves

Today you may be dating a cheater and tomorrow you may be dating a manipulative leech. Regardless of where you stand in your love life, this book will *always* come in handy. If you're single, it will help you avoid the typical booby traps people fall for in the name of love. If you're in a relationship, it'll guide you through dealing with the issues at hand. And there's a little something for you psychos out there as well: getting over exes and irrational obsessions.

♥

So let's cut all the bullshit and take this painful journey together. The sooner you come to terms with reality, the sooner you can move on and enjoy your life. And believe me, I'm the last person to preach about rainbows and butterflies, but there is a life out there worth living. You're just missing out because you're too busy feeding into your delusions.

Stop repeating the same mistakes over and over again and let yourself be happy.

1. Your Biggest Enemy

When you were a kid, your entire world revolved around the power of your mind. You fought dragons, you lived in castles, and you had imaginary friends. And when you were a kid, a wild imagination was actually encouraged. But now that you're an adult the rules have changed.

Technically, you still house all the imagination you had when you were a kid. Problem is, you hardly use it to your advantage. Instead of using it to propel yourself forward as an adult, you allow this power to feed your wishful thinking, face planting you into a world of delusions. *How'd we go from dragons to monogamous cheaters?*

Imagination can either be your best friend or it can be your worst enemy. But since you don't know how to use it, it's usually your enemy. And the worst thing it can do is deprive you of 'learning'. Everything you experience in life comes with a lesson and learning from your past makes the future easier to manage. The danger with imagination is that if you don't like the lesson the experience has to offer, your mind is strong enough to change it. And it's all about recollection; you put the puzzle pieces wherever you think they belong.

So what do we do when we don't understand something? Most of us don't go investigate. Instead, we try to fit it into an existing schema of what we understand the definition of love to be. Instead of asking questions, we assume answers. And if something isn't going our way, we do everything in our power to switch its gears toward the path we want it to take.

So really, a lot more goes on in your relationship when you're alone than it does while the two of you are together. Your mind is constantly working, it's constantly grabbing pieces from other puzzles trying to close the gaps left by the pieces you've lost.

You are your biggest enemy.

Why Delusions are Poisonous...and Pointless

Personally, I think this section needs no explanation but for the sake of argument let's assume you are aware of your delusional state and that you will defend it to your death because it keeps you happy.

Let's do drugs. Imagine being on magic mushrooms. Once the drug hits, you're convinced you're in a world filled with gnomes and purple rain, following fairies down a candle lit path to a magical kingdom. As you dance your way towards the light, you feel nothing but utter euphoria- such wonderful magic mushrooms those were, right? Well, while your mind is there, your body is running full speed into a busy freeway. *Do you see where I'm getting at?*

Delusions don't change reality; they just make it easier to cope with. A delusion is like morphine; it numbs the pain but doesn't make the bruises and open wounds disappear. If you can catch yourself falling deep into a world of gnomes and fairies, then be thankful you haven't overdosed and that you still have a chance to make it out alive. Because if you've ever done drugs, you'll know that the higher the drug takes you, the harder the come down is afterwards. And no one likes the come-down, so stop doing drugs.

There's no point in injecting yourself with something that does you terrible harm and only temporarily numbs the pain. I'm urging you to seek alternative treatment, grow some balls and take it like a champ, au natural. Rid yourself of any reliance on numbing agents that simply cover up the problem without dealing with the cause. Because if you don't, you'll never heal.

Fearing Solitude

Having an affair with your imagination isn't the stupidest thing you could do. Getting into a relationship because you're afraid of being alone is. This is one of the most common reasons people start relationships and stay in them when they know they deserve better.

How often have you caught yourself pardoning asshole behavior from your significant other instead of saying to yourself, "Wait a second. I deserve better than to be treated like this!" But we do it. We accept those behaviors because we think, *better to be with someone than to take on life alone.*

The fear of being alone is a lot more common than you think. You may be the odd ball who's gone through life single and happy, but even you have that friend who has gone from partner to partner without a breath in between. Unfortunately, you gain absolutely nothing by keeping someone at your side that has no business being there - only pain and suffering.

Let's take a look at why we're so scared to be left alone. Is it because we're taught early on about marriage and the role it's supposed to play in our lives? Do you think that if you get a head start in the game it will be a lot easier to find your match? Or maybe you think if you force a relationship to last a certain amount of time it's a guaranteed marriage proposal. When laid out, it all sounds a bit ridiculous, doesn't it?

You shouldn't find someone fit enough to marry; you should marry the one you realize fits you. This isn't a poorly written story in a history book. We have been freed from arranged marriages and we should damn well take advantage of it.

It's that puzzle we were talking about earlier. You can't just bring in pieces from another puzzle and try to make them fit. The goal is to find the puzzle you want to work on, sit down, and get to work with the pieces you already have. It's going to take time, focus, and dedication but the outcome will be one beautiful, gapless masterpiece.

Perhaps you're scared to be alone because you think having someone there is going to make life's little obstacles easier to overcome. This theory is somewhat correct, but not entirely. The right partner *will* support you and help you find the strength within yourself to conquer challenges. Your partner will not, however, hold your hand while you keep your eyes closed and guide you through the maze of life. You might make it out alive but you won't have learned the valuable lessons that come with each hardship, and you'll have to repeat a similar yet harder maze down the line, alone.

The severity of life's obstacles will remain the same no matter what your marital status is. Don't be fooled into thinking that forcing someone to be your sidekick will shorten the journey. With the right partner, it'll be easier, but only because they will help you on the path of self-discovery.

Selfishness Vs. Compromise

From a very early age, we're taught that being selfish is a punishable behavior. "Share your toys, work together, and give everyone a chance on the swing" should echo the memories of your childhood.

At that point of our lives, being selfish was never okay. Part of growing up, however, is learning when to put ourselves first and when to cater to the needs of others. Unfortunately, we hardly ever get the situations right. We're either constantly demanding the most irrational things, or we end up doormats to those who don't deserve us. *How the hell are we supposed to find our way back to the middle?*

We begin by understanding the difference between selfishness and compromise. When you're selfish, you want everything to go your way and believe you deserve to have everything you want. You don't consider the other's needs or desires; you simply assume they're worth less than your own. Whatever you want is non-negotiable and you're unwilling to budge.

When you compromise, on the other hand, you consider the situation as objectively as possible and sometimes give up your wants and desires so that your partner can be happy too. It takes a bigger person to be able to compromise, but it's important to remember that in most cases, both parties are giving *something* up for the sake of the relationship.

Being selfish isn't always a bad thing. The best time to be selfish, in fact, is during the process of discovering your mate. You have to be able to sit down with yourself and single out what you consider to be non-negotiable qualities *before* you're actually in the relationship. If, for example, you know you're a career oriented person who devotes a good chunk of your day to working, don't hook up with someone who's got an obvious cling factor and doesn't have as much of a demanding lifestyle. At some point, the two differences *will* collide and burn the relationship to the ground. Make a list if it helps, but know that this is an important base to any healthy relationship.

When is being selfish a bad thing? Let's use the career-oriented example. Imagine you meet this fantastic person and right from the get-go they tell you that their job is their number one priority. You smile, nod, and convince yourself that this is something you'll be okay with because, let's face it, you're getting a total package in return. If this isn't something you are genuinely okay with, however, it'll end up biting you in the ass in the middle of the relationship. You'll find yourself demanding that your lover spends more time with you and less with work. Before you know it, you'll no longer recognize yourself.

A relationship is no place for either party to be selfish; if you're still living life at that selfish stage, you're just not ready for a relationship. A relationship is the joining of two separate lives and you've got to remember that the two lives won't always flow smoothly side-by-side. There will be times when the two will cross, and one of you will need to back up in order to get you both flowing again.

If compromises are hard for you to consider and, say, you're used to being an only child and always getting what you want, there are ways to make it easier. Note that every time you cave in, it'll make it easier for your partner to do the same for you. It becomes easier to please one another because you know your partner is working just as hard as you are at making it work. But compromise should go both ways. If you catch yourself constantly caving while your partner continues to get it his/her way, you're becoming a doormat. Compromise is a two way street. If you don't see your partner heading in your direction, it's best to turn around and change routes.

Understanding the difference between selfishness and compromise is crucial; and so is realizing that both have a time and place within a relationship. *Beware.*

Letting Go of Your Past

Most of us will go through many relationships in our lifetimes; some will be great and others will suck. Regardless of the outcome, each relationship is meant to be a step on the learning ladder. It's a filter process to help you decode what you *really* want in a partner, and it's important.

But knowing that it's part of life doesn't make the break up any easier, does it? We get so emotionally wrapped up in every relationship that it's inevitable for us to carry some of our past into our future. The trick is to learn to keep it to yourself. Comparing today to yesterday is a recipe for disaster, no matter what the situation because no tomorrow will ever be like today.

Wondering how your inability to let go of the past can hurt your relationship? Well, let's assume your last lover left a particularly bad taste in your mouth and that you consider the whole thing to have been an epic failure. That's fine; most of our past relationships are, anyway. If you haven't let go, however, you'll bring your fear of history repeating itself into your new life – undeserved.

When you're haunted by your past, you respond to situations that don't exist. For example, you might call your new lover a cheater because your dinner plans are being canceled for a business meeting. When really, it was your ex that banged the secretary and this new person in your life is actually in talks of getting a promotion. You're reacting to something that isn't happening. Not only do you appear crazy, but this is also a sure way to push potential mates away.

Holding on to a rainbow and butterfly filled past is just as damaging as holding on to a negative one. You set standards for your new partner without realizing they're all virtually impossible to meet. The best example I can use is for you to pretend that the two lovers, past and present, speak different languages. If you were to demand a book report on Romeo and Juliet, a French essay and a Chinese essay would look completely different. But, just because they're different doesn't mean one is delivering any less of a book report. People have different ways of displaying love; it's unfair to demand one to be like another. Just like the days, no two are ever the same.

You have to realize that your new partner is not your ex. Although you may be someone that always falls in love with a specific type, there are still many qualities that set people apart from each other. It's important you do everything in your power to keep your past and your present from blending into one unrecognizable reality.

The Cling Factor

Being clingy and possessive is a surefire way to ruin something, regardless of whether or not it ever had a chance to survive. We often don't catch ourselves doing it, but being overly attached is a lot more common than you think. It doesn't have to reach extreme *Fatal Attrac-*

tion levels, either. It can be something as simple as demanding an hourly phone call or wanting to be attached at the hip every minute of the day. Regardless of the extremity, being clingy is a no-win situation; you think you're holding your partner close, when in reality you couldn't be pushing them further away.

When you're in a relationship you're entitled to a few a things: the first being privacy. You are not given a pass to go through emails and panty drawers just because you've won the title of boyfriend or girlfriend. Cell phones are off limits and you have no right to demand passwords or pass codes to your partner's private accounts. If this is hard for you to accept or even understand, you may very well be a danger to yourself and to those around you.

Just because you're shacking up, doesn't mean you're expected to give your friends up, either. For you to demand that of your partner makes you insane. You are an addition to his/her life; you haven't taken it over. Romance and friendship are both equally vital to the sanity and happiness of an individual. Know your part, accept it, and go make some friends of your own.

On that note, being in a relationship doesn't mean that you're expected to give up *any* part of your life – other than the obvious like sleeping with other people, for example. A relationship is the joining of two lives, but they still remain just that: *two lives*.

Your partner is entitled to go out with friends, continue attending weekly happy hour sessions, and have a social life without having to be attached to your hip. It also goes without saying that your partner is not expected to report his or her every move to you. A headcount of the previous evening's festivities is unnecessary, as is an immediate response to every text, call, or email. Remember that people have jobs and that they don't want to be the one to say, "Oh I'm sorry about that, it was just my cling machine of a lover."

If you can't stop your clingy, possessive behavior you risk losing your relationship before it even has the chance to take off. You have to trust that your partner is with you because he or she loves you, and that won't change simply because you're not receiving an hourly reminder. *The smaller the cage you hold your lover in, the harder he or she will fight to get out.*

And if your partner is, for whatever reason, okay with your possessive behavior, don't think you're in the clear. Two fuck-ups don't make a healthy relationship. Accepting possessive behavior is a sign of major issues, too. If left unresolved, the two can combine for an ultimate combustion; and it will not end well. If this sounds like you, skip forward to Chapter 11. You'll both leave scarred, confused, and in terrible pain. Clinginess kills relationships.

Obstacles

Regardless of which of the above rings a bell, each can prove to be a major obstacle in achieving a healthy relationship. And what do they have in common? They all have to do with you.

These issues can contribute to your inability to see things for what they are. If you're diving into the waters of love with all of the wrong gear, drowning is inevitable. Realize none of the above is anything to be ashamed of, just take a step back and deal with it before you involve the heart of someone else.

Without realizing it, you've become your biggest enemy. You should be able to rely on yourself for the necessary drop of sanity when you feel like you're in too deep. How can you trust yourself if even your own intentions aren't clear?

If I've learned one thing in life, it's to always put yourself first. Essentially, you're the only common denominator guaranteed to be there for every moment of your life. Friends, lovers, and even family members aren't guaranteed pieces to your puzzle. Put as many resources into making yourself the best version of you possible.

2. Letting Go of Perfection

Somewhere between fairy tales and 80s chick flicks we got a pretty screwed up idea of what love is *supposed* to look like. Images of the guy holding a boom box outside our window imprinted themselves in our vulnerable little brains and we assume all marriage proposals should came standard with rose petals and candlelit pathways to steaming hot baths. Suddenly, our ordinary little relationships aren't quite good enough anymore. *What happened?*

Sure, it's easy to blame romantic comedies and those highly addictive romance novels we order online because we're too embarrassed to purchase them in public. But we're not so easily influenced when it comes to Sci-fi or murder mysteries, are we? The truth is, a basic, fundamental trace of wishful thinking has to exist in order for us to truly put our eggs in that perfect relationship basket; and it does. So incorporate that innate hunger with the envy of your sister's *perfect* relationship and you've got a recipe for your newfound love affair with perfection.

Through one outlet or another we've gotten trained to know love before we experience it; to expect things of future partners we've never even met, and to settle for nothing less than a storybook ending. The problem is, reality hardly ever plays out that way. While the standard qualities like respectful, loving, and supportive universally apply, you'd be surprised to find what really attracts you to your partner the most are all the rare, unspoken, unexpected qualities.

The Perfect Mate

Don't give up hope. Perfection still exists; you just can't find it in fairytale books and John Cusack movies. The definition of perfection is reliant on the person defining it. A quick glance at a typical Happy Hour group of friends might help explain this theory.

The Business Pal: Career oriented and driven, whose idea of perfection is someone who has climbed the corporate ladder holding his or her ambitions tightly between clenched teeth.

The Artist: With the appreciation of all things art, the artist seeks to be challenged and constantly enlightened.

The Hopeless Romantic: Addicted to all predefined notions of love, this heartbroken pal wants a storybook character to come to life and exist solely to fulfill all existing romantic clichés.

The Slut: Legs are spread and zippers are undone. This friend wants nothing less than the shortest of commitments and the longest of privates - and isn't shy about it.

I could go on, but I'm assuming you get the point. Present each pal with another pal's idea of the perfect mate and witness all hell break loose. So who is this 'perfect' person supposed to complement, the artist or the slut? Perfection is in the eye of the beholder; it mirrors the needs and desires of an individual rather than those of the masses.

It's also worth noting that not everyone's idea of a perfect mate is a healthy one. For example, someone may need a partner who is more like a parental figure than a lover. Most of us can agree, however, that a romantic relationship is no place to deal with your daddy issues. But that might be this person's idea of perfection. *Is it yours?*

Letting go of these expectations when finding someone new will help the relationship proceed much more smoothly than you could have ever imagined. You may not even be conscious of the fact you're holding these predefined notions in your head, but they're still there, gnawing at those little 'imperfections.' Regardless, they will almost always float to the surface to bite you in the ass, so when you decide to let them go, make sure they're really gone.

The Perfect Relationship

By now you *should* know that no two relationships are alike. If no two relationships are alike, one can deduce that the 'ideal' relationship cannot in fact exist. You may envy your friend and how romantic her boyfriend is, but you'll find his infatuation with video games borderline repulsive while she finds it irresistibly amusing. Or maybe your guy friend has the hottest girlfriend who turns heads wherever she goes, but her high-pitched, seal-like voice haunts you in your sleep every time you see her. Your friend, on the other hand, masturbates to it.

Nothing is ever "perfect" to the naked eye, and if you're comfortable defending another relationship as perfect, you're either not looking hard enough or you're in a drug-induced state of denial.

Couples need to fight. If you're not fighting, you're not moving forward. If you let everything pass, you're either a coward or you don't care. When you love someone, that someone's actions affect you. You *have* to react, one way or another. To remain indifferent isn't normal. Real couples will do everything in their power not to fight but there will be times that feelings cannot be contained. So, this idea that a perfect relationship is always rainbows and butterflies is a load of shit. What matters is how you deal with conflict and how you move forward after a dispute.

There is no guidebook that says you're supposed to be making love X amount of times a week. Every couple is different. Some couples shag every day, others do it once a week. Some even have to pencil it into their calendar of activities. If there were a predefined number of shags you should complete per week in order to consider your relationship healthy, most of us would be screwed - figuratively, of course.

Something else that's misunderstood: the amount of time the two of you should be spending together. No couple should be attached at the hip; it's a recipe for disaster. But besides being completely dependent on one another, the amount of time a couple spends together is deemed ideal by them, and only them. Some couples can't stand to be apart, while others need their space.

Lastly, I think it's common knowledge that not having everything in common isn't necessarily a death sentence for your new developing relationship. Not only can that get quite boring, but at some point one party is going to demand something new and exciting. So if you find you have different tastes in music, or that while you're into art, he's into sports, don't despair; you still have a chance to survive.

In other words, everyone has a different way of defining perfection and that's the way it should remain. My parents no longer sleep in the same room, let alone the same bed, and they're one of the happiest married couples I know. He snores and she wrestles the bed-sheets; their recipe for perfection includes a good night's sleep. And what about the couple who doesn't talk over dinner? Does that mean they've run out of things to say and have let their relationship run its course? No. Maybe they like dinnertime to be a time to silently reflect of the day's activities, in good company.

The Love Story

What is another way fables and romances have royally fucked us? The damn love story. We're tricked into believing that it must follow certain guidelines in order to truly be romantic and campfire worthy. If its beginning isn't poetic, the relationship's credibility is put to question and is suddenly expected to crash and burn.

Like, for example, the story of how you two met. Maybe your soon-to-be boyfriend didn't introduce himself by asking you to throw down your hair from your bedroom balcony. So what? No one ever tells you that you might meet your soulmate in jail; that wouldn't make for the best bedtime story, would it? In fact, the story of how you two met is hardly ever out of a storybook. But don't despair.

Just because you can't brag about having met the

love of your life while feeding starving children in Uganda, doesn't mean your story is not worth telling. Nowadays, most people meet online. They meet at the Laundromat, and in line for the unisex bathroom stall at the corner gas station. What's important is that the story makes euphoria flow through *your* veins every time you tell it. And if you're in love, meeting your partner while recycling cans will feel as romantic as meeting while climbing Mount Everest.

The Sequence of Things

Blame the 50s and your grandmother's strong desire to keep tradition alive; somewhere down the line we got introduced to our very own 8 Steps Towards Your White Picket Fence. The question is, how much of it still holds true for you?

OLD RULES: 8 Steps Towards Your White Picket Fence

1. **First Date:** Ladies, wait to be approached. Gentlemen, be polite in your inquiries. Keep it safe with dinner and a movie and talk about your favorite hobbies. Limit your alcohol intake! Wouldn't want to come off being too limber.

2. **Casual Dating:** Best to take your time with these things. First kiss, walk to the front door and hope you're free to catch dinner and a movie next Friday night. You might mention you're dating to your group of friends but introductions will have to wait until it's official!

17

3. **Go Steady:** Time to take it to the next level! You have the talk and become exclusive. This stage includes all introductions and even the occasional public group appearance. Girls, this is when you're allowed to start doodling his name on your notebook.

4. **Engagement:** Ask for her hand in marriage. Make sure to go through the traditional route and just pray the sucking up has worked. Once it's been publicly announced, the engagement should follow the standard year long run before all the wedding planning comes to life.

5. **Marriage:** After thousands of dollars have been spent on the right location, the right wedding planner and the right center pieces, it's time to become Husband and Wife in front of *all* your loved (and not so loved) ones.

6. **New House:** That she obviously hasn't seen yet but you carefully picked out just for her! The house comes standard with extra bedroom that will someday become the nursery. Don't forget the garden and the kitchen island! And if you get one with a white picket fence too, you're set!

7. **Get the Puppy:** Now that you're married you won't have to worry about sharing custody of your new puppy if things happen to crash and burn. Starting off with a puppy is a great way to test the waters and see where the two of you stand in regards to starting a family.

8. **Make the Baby:** Enough practice! Let's do it!

While many still honor the value of tradition, things have become a bit more complex, redefining what we know as the American Dream. Women are working, contraceptives are failing, economies are crashing, and members of the same sex are suddenly falling in love and demanding equal rights! What has this world come to? Progress, that's what. Needless to say, the rules have been redefined accordingly. The white picket fence may no longer be our dream destination.

NEW RULES: 8 Steps Towards Happiness

1. **First Date:** We've gone crazy and challenged the norm: dinner and a movie is no longer our go-to adventure for a first date. Add bar hopping, zip lining, or a trip to the zoo to spice shit up. Also, women are stepping up to the plate by expressing interest in potential suitors and asking them out instead.

2. **Casual Dating:** We're too obsessed and too impatient. Give us a couple of dates and a good time between the sheets and that's all we need. We're suddenly offended when we find out someone we're casually dating is seeing other people. Yet we still need our friends to approve before we get too serious. Casual dating is an exhilarating and uncertain clusterfuck...and we're obsessed.

3. **Relationships:** Going steady used to consist of, at the very least, feeling that your lover *might* be 'the one'. In some cases today, it still does. But now we dive in without even considering the thought of a future together. Heck, some of us even *know* it won't go anywhere and we still don't care. Sex has already happened, sometimes as early as the first date. And meeting the parents can happen as late as after the proposal. Or never at all.

4. **Engagement:** Parental permission is a tradition slowly fading away, especially because engagements can be broken and can happen multiple times with multiple people. There is no specified waiting period either; proposals can be made as early as the first week together or never at all. And they can last anywhere from an hour to an eternity.

5. **Marriage:** Today, there are alternatives to marrying in a church. There are plenty of portals for the Do-It-Yourselfers. If steering away from tradition is the rebellion you crave, there's always Las Vegas. The vision of the lavish traditional wedding is blurred and you can have just as much of a meaningful marriage by opting for a civil ceremony instead. Oh… and some couples don't *ever* get married but stay together forever.

6. **New House:** The woman hasn't approved of the house? *Yeah, right.* Today, most couples make these big decisions together. (Not to mention the bank will need both of you in order to give you a loan.) And if a woman isn't happy with the po-

tential home you're considering, you better have a list of other choices ready to show her. Couples are usually already cohabitating before they get married. In this fucked up economy it becomes more about what you can afford, rather than the picket fence around the 'yard'.

7. **Pets:** Pets are usually already there. Either they're carried over from your single life or they're acquired mid-relationship. Some couples never even get a pet, especially since some places charge pet rent. *Dicks.*

8. **Babies:** Unplanned pregnancies happen, contraceptives fail, and children are carried over from previous relationships. Some pregnancies are planned before the ring, while others are prevented all together.

While the New Rules may be a little hard to swallow, they're the reality of today. Aiming for a white picket fence is pointless because the proverbial white picket fence no longer exists.

The point is to create your own dream and follow it, creating your own rules along the way. Don't hesitate to switch a couple of steps and do things 'out of order.' The goal is to reach your definition of happiness, no one else's.

♥

So who the hell defines perfection? The answer is no one but yourself. That's why Chapter 1 is so important. You've got to figure out what you want in life first. Do *you* want children? Is the potential and timing of marriage reliant on *you* achieving your career goals? Ask yourself these questions and know the answers before a potential suitor comes along and asks them. Remember that you're allowed to do things out of order and skip any steps you don't want to experience. *It's ok!*

Allow yourself to go through the motions, let go of relationships that are doomed to fail –because 99% of them are- and gather what lessons you can from each one. Know what you're willing to compromise so there is no dispute about it when a new relationship begins.

Allow perfection to consist of different traits and remain open to new suggestions. If you don't stop chasing those preconceived ideals, you'll be too busy to notice what makes your potential partner unique, and even perhaps the yin to your yang.

Perfection is constructed along the way and there is no possible way for you to prepare for it before its arrival. If you don't let go of this ill-founded idea of perfection, you'll be paving a road full of disappointments and shattered expectations.

The 9 Mirages of Love

The 9 Mirages of Love

3. The Affair

There's a good chance that at some point in your life you'll be 'the other' person in an affair. I'm not saying everyone is destined to be involved in an affair; all I'm saying is that it happens more than you know. You'd be surprised how many people you know are guilty of it and have simply decided to not share their experiences. The small fraction of you who never dabble in such sin will have to be the one being cheated on – pick your poison.

But I'm not here to bash your behavior, judge your moral standing, or go tell your mommy what a whore you've been. The reality is that affairs happen, and sometimes we're not on the good side.

There are many reasons you may find yourself in an affair. Sometimes, you don't know; others you don't care; but mostly, you are merely a slave to wishful thinking.

Falling Victim to Broken Promises

This is, by far, the most common scenario. You meet someone you fall head over heels for, who claims to reciprocate the feelings, and you're convinced you've just found your soulmate. Discovering that they've already been spoken for seems like an easy hurdle to surpass. *It was just bad timing, of course!* The fact you're constantly reassured that the two of you will 'someday' be together only contributes to the delusion. Little do you know that falling for a married, or otherwise involved person, is like asking to be gang banged and left on the side of the street.

First of all, it's important to remember that these 'lovers' are having their cake and eating it too. Why would they give it up? They're having the best of both worlds and they'll usually do whatever it takes to keep it that way. Meanwhile, you're left victim to constant wishful thinking and broken promises.

It doesn't matter whether or not the intention of leaving really exists. These cheaters are going to dish out whatever promises they have to in order to keep you in their bed. *Lies.* Some may even feel guilty about lying and might begin to believe they'd actually consider leaving their partner. Regardless, you can rest assured that 9 times out of 10 it's utter bullshit.

Even if it's not and they genuinely believe they would leave their partner, they never do. They are chicken shit when they begin the affair; what makes you think they will suddenly grow a pair and own up to their infidelities? As time passes, the excuses will keep coming. Either it's not the right time or it'll be easier once the kids are gone or… blah, blah, blah. *It will never end.*

The truth is you're being used. The moment you fell for the first excuse was the moment there was a complete power shift. You genuinely believe you two met at the right place at the wrong time. The passion between you is so intense, you can't help but believe you're soulmates. You become so delusional that you even ignore the possibility that this 'passion' is only a result of the fact your affair is forbidden. You ignore the complexities of breaking up a family or a serious committed relationship because you are certain it's the two of you that are meant to build a future. You've disappeared into a world of denial and you're willing to wait as long as it takes to be with the one you love.

By now, you should realize how foolish you look; fucking ridiculous, right? Deep down, you know things aren't going to change. You know words hold no weight and that you're the only reason this affair is still going on. Remember… you have the power to end it.

Why the Affair?

At some point, you need to step out of the situation and ask yourself the hard-hitting question, "Why am I here?" You'd be surprised where an hour of contemplation will lead you. Is it the person that you're attracted to? Or is it the chase for the unattainable? Perhaps it can be a little bit of both, but at least one of them has got to ring a bell.

Person

Most 'other' people in affairs will fool themselves into believing their "previously committed" lovers are perfect. But surely, the fact they're cheating on their spouses can't be *that* admirable, can it? Unless you can openly admit that lying and deceit turn you on, you're in denial about this supposed 'perfection.'

Unfortunately, in these situations love and infatuation are as real as they come and there's nothing anyone can say or do to change your mind – not even tell you your lover's in it for the bang. But ask yourself, what would you say to a friend in the same position?

Next, you need to ask yourself whether it's *who the person is* that's feeding your attachment, or if it's *how they make you feel*. During the scope of your love life it's common to get the two mixed up; it doesn't just take an affair. And even though it's not going to solve your problem, it's important you make that distinction.

If you're in love with the person, the infatuation will remain and you'll forever be stuck in lala land. Because, as stated before, it doesn't matter what anyone says to you, you will be dead set on defending the name of your future soulmate – no matter what it takes.

If it's how the person makes you feel and it's euphoric, why would you want to give that up? It's really easy to word vomit the perfect promises without having to be held accountable, especially if you're butt naked in the back of a BMW.

The 'other' woman get's treated like a princess, which makes it hard for her to resist the affair. And if you're the 'other' man, all the cheater has to tell you is that you're better in bed than her boyfriend is.

The cheater makes you feel like a rare gem and you suddenly forget the fact you've become the bitch on the side.

The Chase

This situation has your ego written all over it. Maybe the idea of the forbidden fruit turns you on. Perhaps you aim for the unattainable because it's a challenge you feel the need to conquer. Regardless, it has nothing to do with the person or the relationship you're breaking up; this whole ordeal revolves around *you*.

Maybe you've just been dumped and you now have something to prove. How could your partner just *leave* knowing there are others out there willing to jeopardize their already existing relationships to be with you?

It doesn't matter what area of your ego needs to be stroked; this route will only give you short-lived satisfaction. Once the rush passes, you'll be left with yet another gash to your ego to heal: the home-wrecker gash. Affairs are complicated enough, there's no need to egg one on in the name of low self-esteem.

Unfortunately, it's usually these 'thrill of the chase' affairs that manage to break marriages and committed relationships apart. In other words, it's when you're in it for the ride that your lover calls you in the middle of the night and says, "Baby! I did it! I'm free! Now we can be together!" Suddenly, this cheating fuck is your responsibility and you're expected to start and maintain a healthy relationship. *Good luck, you deserve it!*

When You Become the Psycho

It's easy to end up in the broken hearted, scorned lover role. It's also easy to get bat-shit crazy because of it. The passion is so strong between you that you feel your actions are justified. Unfortunately, they're not. Being the crazy 'other' isn't going to get you what you want.

The shit usually hits the fan when your lover tells you his or her current relationship is the only thing standing between the two of you being together.

You find yourself daydreaming about slashing your lover's partner's tires and leaving a letter with the words, "Back up, bitch!" on the windshield. *Classy.* Daydreaming is normal; letting those dreams become a reality is not. But you think this will prove your devotion to your lover and finally prove you're in it for the long run. All in the name of true love, right? *Psycho.*

Threatening and/or demanding won't get things moving any quicker than they would if your lover really wanted to be with you. First of all, you'll forever be branded a psycho. Secondly, you've got to realize that not being loud enough *is not* the reason things aren't changing; things aren't changing because they simply aren't going to.

If someone wants to be with you, they'll make it happen. The feelings will overcome the complexities of standing relationships, planets will align, and love will conquer all. And, you won't have to pull out the knife to make it happen.

When it Works

I almost don't want to write this in fear that it'll give you false hope. It's *very* rare, but there are times that an affair *can* lead to a successful relationship. I say 'successful' because it's important to remember that there are times a cheater will leave their spouse for a short time and then cowardly go back begging. And don't forget the times that, like regular relationships, you simply realize you weren't meant to be. Needless to say, the odds are against you.

Having said that, it is possible to meet your soulmate while you're with someone else. Maybe you settled down too early in life, or maybe meeting someone new and interesting triggered the realization that your current relationship sucked. If life was as simple as finding someone we mesh with and settling down for good, there would be no need for therapists, love doctors, friends, and most importantly, alcohol. I think it's safe to say all of these things are still in high demand... life is still a mess.

Wondering how you know if it's *really* meant to be? Give it a deadline. This is the *one time* you're allowed to give an ultimatum. Tell yourself and your otherwise "committed lover" that if the two of you aren't together by a certain date, you'll walk. If you're risking your heart, and your dignity, the least you can do is retain as much self respect as possible. Just make sure to follow through with the threat. And remember, you'll be dating a cheater.

Ending it and Getting Out

For the other 99% of you out there currently involved in an affair for all of the wrong reasons, it's time to end it. One thing to keep in mind is that affairs usually happen when there is something missing in the cheater's existing relationship; it's not that you're irresistible; you just provide something the cheater needs.

Provided that you have given the ultimatum and it's been turned down, or ignored, it's time for you to recognize this for what it is: a mirage. Even if the sex is amazing, it doesn't mean the relationship will be too. The words you're being told are easy to ramble when no consequences have to be faced. All you're good for is providing something that person needs at that point in time; you are not relationship material.

Stop daydreaming and realize you've still got a whole life to live. It doesn't matter whether you're in your 20s or your 50s. Giving life a chance has got to be better than waiting at someone else's doorstep for the rest of your life. You can experience the world when you allow your focus to wander away from an obsession. Because that's what this is: an obsession.

Find a support group. The Internet is full of online

communities where you can speak freely about your experiences. You might be going through all of this alone because you fear being judged by your friends. And let's face it, many people we consider our friends would find it pretty easy to point fingers. However you do it, you must find an outlet. Because going through this alone is *not* the way you want to go about things. Just like any other break up, you will need a support system, especially if you're really emotionally attached.

Once you've found your support system, it's time to make shit happen. Give yourself a good pep talk in the mirror and when you feel you've lied yourself into oblivion, make a move. The goal is to end *all* contact. You wouldn't believe how often people end affairs and start them right back up after a few short weeks. If you're going through the emotional rollercoaster of actually ending it, make it worth your while. Check out Chapter 13 for further reading.

A lot of affairs happen at work and the no-contact rule doesn't sound like a plausible route. In this case, avoiding contact might tip people off on your relationship. So instead, just scale it back to regular small talk and keep the conversations in public; don't respond to private emails/texts or other attempts to communicate. Before you know it, you might even be able to stop *all* contact without anyone noticing.

When will you be ready to bring the contact back? Whenever you're no longer thinking about it - that's the only time you'll ever be ready. The problem with 'staying in touch' is that you're likely to still be in a vulnerable position. The cheater needs *you*, and they know what you need to hear in order to come crawling back. If you don't give yourself enough time to build that armor, you won't be ready to handle the bullets.

The Breath of Fresh Air

Saying goodbye will be hard. It'll be as painful as any other heartbreak. It will seem like the end of the world, like you missed out on your chance to be with someone you *knew* you were meant to be with. You'll suffer in the same way you always have, fearing this rejection will be the last blow. You'll gain weight or you'll lose it, you'll isolate yourself or go whoring around town. Regardless of how you reach your dark place, you'll get there.

You'll go through the anger phase with a breeze, hating the situation and the fact you were made out to be such a fool. You might even beat yourself up for falling for the unattainable.

And then one day, you'll wake up and things will be a little better. Suddenly, you'll decide to actually get dressed for the day. You'll check your phone a little less than you did the day before and you might even be able to get the situation out of your mind for a little while longer. Although you won't recognize it, this is progress.

Each day will be easier than the last. Time heals all wounds and the day will come where you'll actually start to believe everything you told yourself in the mirror that day; you *do* deserve better. You will no longer hate him/her for having led you to believe there was hope, and most importantly, you'll finally forgive yourself for being the 'other lover'.

4. The Cheater

When cheating occurs in a relationship, the pain is so excruciating that you genuinely believe no one else has ever endured it and gotten out alive. Unfortunately, you're wrong; infidelity has wounded many hearts, broken many relationships and has absolutely no intention of slowing down. In fact, most of us have been guilty of it as well – and if you haven't cheated, chances are you will. Cheating is a natural part of the relationship learning process. And sometimes we just can't help but become slaves to temptation. However, just because it's common doesn't mean it's justified, nor does it make the pain any easier to deal with.

Society puts pressure on us from an early age by bombarding us with images of happy couples. We are taught that marriage and children should be our end goal and such a goal can only be achieved through a stable, monogamous relationship. It may be discrete but it's a substantial pressure nonetheless. We feel forced to jump into things we're not prepared for and sometimes, we fuck up. Still, the person being hurt in the process will never be able to differentiate between good and ill intentions. The stabbing pain of infidelity is never one easily numbed.

We have many different reactions to infidelity. Sometimes we play stupid because it's easier than admitting our relationships are crumbling down in flames. Sometimes we easily forgive because we'd like to believe in those we love. And sometimes we're out the door before the cheater has a chance to say anything at all because we vowed to never forgive such horrendous behavior. So, which reaction is the right one?

Your own moral values play a huge role in how you're going to deal with your partner cheating on you. However, it's important to remember that life isn't black and white. And just like how your last two exes aren't the same person, you should know that neither are you; your experiences have already changed who you are. During each relationship we grow, learn, and change. Give yourself room to adapt to the situation for what it is, rather than being set on your preconceived notion of how you think you should deal with it.

First thing's first: Are you being cheated on?

Initially, I wanted to steer clear of the checklist approach. Later, after going through a bunch of emails from my readers, I had a change of heart. There seems to be a place where suspicion and facts blur. Some mystery line drawn in the sand that separates the two, becoming even harder to find when we're fools in love. Human beings have a complex mind and we're capable of creating some fucked up shit with it. A basic guideline might help clarify an already suspicious situation. But try not to rely on it as a sole agent in determining whether or not your partner is cheating.

Remember: Although some of the following signs are dead giveaways, never jump to conclusions without calmly, not accusingly, approaching your partner. An isolated sign doesn't necessarily mean you're being cheated on; other issues may be at play here, like, for example, your partner may just be over you.

Questionable Behaviors:

1. Your partner acts distant
2. There is an obvious disconnect between you in every day interaction
3. Your partner is suddenly more attentive, almost clingy
4. Your partner constantly picks fights with you
5. Increase of aggressiveness and defensiveness
6. Things are suddenly locked and accounts are suddenly password protected
7. Accuses you of cheating
8. Sudden drastic change in appearance

When it comes to behavior, you're looking for sudden *drastic* changes. Some of us are good at lying verbally but our bodies and behaviors have a harder time adapting. If your partner has always been a private person, you shouldn't be surprised to see his computer prompt for a password at the Log In screen. If, however, you've always shared cell phone contents freely and all of a sudden there's a password locking you out, that's cause for suspicion.

Things You're in Denial About

1. Wrong name called out in bed, multiple times
2. Lipstick smudges, foreign panties and jewelry that doesn't belong to you
3. Secret friends you're not allowed to meet

4. Emails/ Texts/ Photo Exchanges, etc.
5. Dead fish sex

You're probably wondering why the above list was even mentioned. You'd be surprised to know how many people would rather trick themselves into believing everything is okay, rather than having to deal with the possibility that they're relationship is over. Denial is a bitch.

The Approach

So you're pretty sure something is going on and you think you're ready to approach your partner, unarmed, over the whole ordeal. Great. Now what? Put all forms of weapons down; hide that crazy forehead vein you get when you're upset, and use the words that deliver the coldest of chills, "We need to talk."

First things first, you have to prepare yourself for every possible outcome. Your partner may admit to it right away and express no feelings of regret, or you may find your guilty lover on his or her knees begging for forgiveness before you even have a chance to react. On the other hand, the entire thing may turn out to be a figment of your imagination, leaving you to feel like a psychotic, possessive freak. Do as much prep work as possible; it'll help to cushion the fall.

Sometimes, approaching your partner will not give you the results you desire. You may be lied to or you may just not be content in hearing 'no' when your suspicions scream 'yes.' Whatever the reason, your partner is denying any foul play and you're not satisfied with the response. You've got a few choices here:

Leave

If your partner denies foul play, you'll probably remain suspicious. This unexplained suspicion may lead you to feel uncomfortable in your own skin. That is why it's important to remember that despite the lack of concrete evidence, you still have every right to pack your shit and go. Jealousy can do a 180 on your personality and you may not like what it turns you into. Just because you're not physically holding the panties that belong to your lover's mistress doesn't mean you'll start believing work runs late every Friday afternoon.

Stay and Shut Up

You can also choose to accept your partner's response and wait for further cause for suspicion. This option is for the saner bunch. Make sure you're ready to put up with the same gut feelings that led you to question your relationship in the first place. Such a task is out of reach for most of us, considering that once we're emotionally invested it's hard to remain unaffected by their behaviors.

Stay and Beat the Issue Into the Ground

This is dangerous territory that'll either lead to a very unhealthy relationship or drive your partner away, both leaving you to wonder if they had ever even cheated on you in the first place. Until you find concrete evidence, your harassment isn't likely to arise a confession. Once they know you've got some suspicion, the time of confession will come on their own terms, not yours. Keying people's cars and interrogating your partner's friends on his/her whereabouts isn't going to get you an answer any sooner.

When we're in love and obsessed, leaving is a hard thing to do. For some reason, we're addicted to the drama and we tend to confuse an unhealthy relationship for a passionate one. Unfortunately, for people that are this blinded by obsession, even holding those infidelity-stained panties isn't going to make a difference. They're in it for the long haul, regardless.

Types of Cheaters

Once the acts of infidelity are out in the open, it'll be time to face the music. The question is what kind of cheater are you dealing with? Those who have been cheated on multiple times will vouch that no two cases are the same. And although presenting you with only 6 scenarios may leave you feeling cheated, take comfort in knowing that most 'other' scenarios are mere variations of the ones below. Let's see who's in your bed.

The Coward

These cheaters are the ones that no longer want to be with you but are too afraid to say it. In their mind, being caught red handed, along with drastic changes in their behavior, gives you reason to do what they're too scared to do themselves: end the relationship. If you do threaten to end the relationship, you should encounter no struggle on their part.

One Time Offender

These cheaters are generally decent partners and don't usually cause you pain. The one time occurrence may have been a drunken mistake or even a cry for help; indicating that your relationship needs attention. They will most likely come clean on their own and petition for a second chance.

The Genital Collector

The Genital Collector's life is a party of one, and you're nowhere on the guest list. You don't even cross their mind before they dive into bed with someone else. Why? It's all about their ego and their ability to conquer. If a fight is put up when you try to leave, it'll most likely be in fear of a bruised ego, not because they're afraid of losing *you*.

The Emotional Cheater

These cheaters find their actions admirable; refraining from giving in to temptation proves to be a hard feat for others but not for them. But although no physical contact is made, you feel equally betrayed nonetheless. The reasons behind these cheaters' actions may vary: they may be seeking what's missing in your relationship elsewhere or they may be too cowardly to admit your relationship is over. Whether or not they put up a fight will give you further insight on the matter.

The Clueless Cheater

Clueless cheaters don't find anything wrong with their behavior. Assuming boundaries had been drawn and labels clearly stated, you could safely deduce that you're either dealing with a sociopath or someone who grew up in a cult. However, as absurd as this sounds, there *are* people out there who feel they are entitled to do as they please. When threatening to end the relationship you might encounter a fight, but it'll be for your partner's freedom to do as they please, and not for a second chance.

The Adrenaline Junkie

These cheaters thrive on the rush, even when your relationship shows no signs of distress. This is usually due to personal issues outside of your relationship. Ending this one will be difficult because it will have blind-sided you and the cheater will likely put up a fight. Sleeping around while single, though still exciting, doesn't pose as much of a risk as sleeping around while in a relationship. Beware of manipulation and promises of change.

Obviously, not every scenario will go the predictable route. What's important is that you're able to differentiate between the one time offender and the adrenaline junkie that swears you're the only one for them while simultaneously screwing your best friend. And of course, some clueless cheaters might genuinely regret their behavior and change their ways once they realize their actions were wrong. Trust yourself enough to make these distinctions. Once those distinctions are made, you'll be better armed for the next step.

Setting boundaries at the beginning of a relationship is very important. Making the assumption that you and your partner have a shared definition of fidelity is a recipe for disaster. By talking about what constitutes cheating for you ahead of time, you may be saving your relationship from a miserable outcome.

How to Deal

Now that it's all out in the open and you've been able to identify the kind of cheater you're dealing with, you find yourself at a fork in the road: do you stay or do you go?

Leaving

Many have known, from as far back as they can remember, that they would never take back a cheater. If you're one of those people, you'll be one foot out the door before your partner's confession is even complete. But would you believe me if I told you that leaving isn't *always* the answer?

There are situations, such as the one time offender, for example, that shouldn't call for such drastic measures. Especially when they indicate a problem in your relationship that needs to be addressed. Let's say your lives have gotten so hectic that you barely make time for one another anymore and you grew apart. Life happens. It may not necessarily be a reflection of the solidity of your relationship; it may just be outside circumstances. And sometimes, you're just as guilty as your partner is. But, if there is a strong desire to make it work on both ends, and genuine regret from the guilty party, leaving might be jumping the gun.

Forgiveness is as much a part of life as anything else, and unless God has personally touched you, you're just as susceptible to fucking up as anyone else is. Therefore, it'd be wise to consider whether or not you'd be asking for a second chance if the roles were reversed. Especially if your partner has always been a good, attentive lover and has never done you harm. Shit happens.

On the other hand, leaving may be exactly what you *need* to do. For almost every other scenario, leaving should be your go-to choice, but it's usually not. For some reason, people tend to be drawn to those who hurt them, and stick around when it's really best they don't. They rely on wishful thinking and denial to get themselves through the tougher times and hope their love is strong enough to conquer everything else. Unfortunately, in most cases, you will NOT be the one to change the error of your partner's ways. And when dealing with cheaters like a genital collector, you best be on your way.

Staying

Staying is often harder to do than leaving. When you leave, although directly more painful because of your partner's absence, you're physically removed from the situation and are able to heal accordingly – no matter how long it takes. Staying implies a constant reminder of your partner's infidelity as well as the need to deal with issues of trust before anything else can progress.

So it's important to ask yourself why you're staying. Are you still there because you're hoping after all those times, *this* one will be the last? Are you staying because you're afraid to leave or afraid to be alone? Are you addicted to your partner in an unhealthy manner? Or are you staying because you genuinely believe the two of you could work this out? If you're considering staying for any reason but the last, you need to leave.

If you do give it a shot, consider relationship counseling. I know many people huff and puff at the idea but you'd be surprised to know that it can make a world of difference. Forgiveness is important but it's hard to achieve when you've been wounded so deeply; it takes a lot of time and a lot of hard work. And although you may believe your love will conquer all, images of infidelity are marked with the darkest of colors that are hard to erase. Counseling also helps you work on your communication skills – a key component to a healthy relationship.

You may also wonder whether your partner is begging to be forgiven out of genuine regret or out of irreparable guilt. To check, make sure you're vocal about what it means to give your relationship a second chance. For example, say, "It will take the both of us to reconstruct this relationship. It will take a lot of time and energy; it'll be hard work. If you're asking to come back out of guilt, take this opportunity as a way out. Save us both from dealing with this same issue again down the line." It's important to remain strong but present the reconstruction as what it really is: hard work.

Lastly, once you forgive, you forgive. You have no right to use your partner's mistakes against them once they've been forgiven. If you can't help it, it may inhibit the relationship from growing any further. And then it'll be your fault, not your partner's.

What You Don't Deserve

Although cheating is a part of life and in some cases should be forgiven, it does not mean you're signing up to become someone's punching bag. There's a fine line between forgiving someone and becoming a doormat. If you find yourself in a situation where you're being repeatedly hurt, you need to look in the mirror and know that you deserve better.

When people do you wrong they'll feel the need to feed you bullshit in hopes of saving their own ass. While it makes it easier for them to sleep at night, it only feeds your vulnerability, leading you to comfortably dive into delusional thinking. You'll find yourself justifying your partner's behavior and before you know it, you'll be telling your friends and family that you know things will change. Soon enough, you'll start to believe it too.

Meanwhile, people will look at you with sadness in their eyes and those that are interested in you won't step foot near you; but you'll be in too deep to understand. Love is a powerful drug and it will make you believe anything you want to in order to keep the high alive.

Little do you know that while you're investing all of your resources into this failed relationship, you're missing out on a whole world of experiences. There are so many phenomenal individuals out there – most that will never dream of hurting you. There is love to experience that you have yet to encounter.

People can change, yes, but it's never when we need them to. You can wait around as long as you want but it's not going to get any better. So believe me when I tell you, you do not deserve this and you are worth more than the low self-esteem and thousands of lost tears. Give yourself to someone who deserves you.

5. Words Like Knives

You don't have to be cheated on to be hurt in a relationship. In fact, the most common, reoccurring pain comes from behaviors we ignore 'in the name of love'. Cruelty doesn't require yelling, abuse isn't always in the form of physical contact, and sometimes you can feel betrayed even when your partner hasn't technically done anything wrong. The pain is the same, so *why don't we treat it as such?*

There are times people hurt others without realizing it. This chapter doesn't apply to those one-time offenders who are generally attentive and kind in all other aspects of the relationship. In such cases, it's up to you to get your ass out of your comfort zone and initiate the conversation; let your partner know how you feel and that you'd like him or her to stop doing whatever it is that's hurting you. If the pain was inflicted involuntarily, stopping the behavior shouldn't be a problem.

This chapter is for those people in relationships where such behavior is not only accepted by the victim but also often justified by the abuser. Before you know it, you're defending his or her behavior to your friends and family, and crying yourself to sleep every other night. *That's a fairytale if I've ever heard one.*

Let's begin by identifying the different situations. Much like other chapters, it's important to remember that although I may not list your specific scenario, it's likely to be a variation of one I *do* list. I've also included some stories from friends and readers to help you relate. See, you're not a piece of shit; we've all been there.

The Sharpest Blades

That Meddling Opposite Sex

When you blame the presence of a third party *on* that third party, you fail to recognize your partner's involvement in the situation. This section isn't about cheating – there's a whole chapter dedicated to infidelity - it's about everything that happens before it.

Imagine you've been waiting all day to see your lover so you brag about your new job promotion. Only, when he or she walks through the door you are unable to get a word in because of their continual yapping about a new 'friend' who happens to not only be witty and funny, but also insanely irresistible and the new catch around the office. While there's nothing wrong with keeping your partner up to speed with the latest office gossip, it's important to know when to draw the line. The green-eyed jealousy monster begins to rear its ugly head when the yapping turns into a never-ending biography about this new outsider.

Monique* and I were catching up over our usual Friday cocktails when she broke out into a panic. "I've been a pretty cool girlfriend, I never give him shit for having so many fucking chick friends but this girl makes me nervous." Her boyfriend had made it clear when they had started dating that he had a lot of female friends and in order for their relationship to work, Monique had to be 'cool' about it.

And on this topic, I'll personally vouch that Monique had been *beyond* 'cool'.

"Her name is something stupid, like Annabelle," she said while taking a huge swig of her vodka soda. "At first, I shrugged her off as another front desk girl that would barely survive a week. But Derrick just wouldn't stop talking about her," she moaned. "He told me *every* guy in the office is trying to go out with her and they're all coming to him because the two of them are friends."

I listened carefully, and made sure not to interrupt. By this point, Monique was starting to get pretty frantic.

"They go out to lunch every day, just the two of them. She bought him a fucking belt because apparently, they have an inside joke going... about fucking belts. I asked him about it and he told me I wouldn't get it." Then she paused. Her eyes filled with tears and she continued, "I tried to tell him about my promotion the other night and he stopped listening because he had gotten a text from her."

She was now crying, in public. "How the hell am I supposed to remain the 'cool' down to earth girlfriend when I'm clearly not okay with this? It's bullshit. I'm losing him but I know that if I say anything he'll just call me psycho and detach even more!"

Now remember: men and women CAN just be friends. In fact, the more confident and sure of yourself you are, the less likely your partner is to stray. The problem isn't your partner being surrounded by the opposite sex; it's his or her inability to note your discomfort. In some cases, it's even done on purpose.

The only way to solve the issue is by talking about it. When approaching your partner, it's a good idea to ask how he or she would feel if the roles were reversed. This trick works in many sticky situations – fold it up and keep it in your back pocket. If all else fails, be vocal about how uncomfortable it makes you feel and that you'd like him or her to stop.

Reality Slap: Human beings are insecure. Period. Rare is the individual sure of himself in every aspect of life. Beware that if you make your feelings known and your partner doesn't stop the brag parade, there's a good chance he or she is doing it on purpose and somehow getting a thrill from it having such an effect on you.

Not Invited, Again

Being attached at the hip is a sure way to screw a relationship up - no matter how close you are. We all need own space, our own friends, and our own life to tap into for quick escapes. When you're in a healthy relationship there are times you invite your partner to join, and there are times you opt to fly solo. This section isn't about accepting the invitation to join; it's about never getting one to begin with.

Take Matt*, for example. He wrote me a few months back, asking if I found his girlfriend's behavior suspicious. They had been dating for about 3 months and were long passed the

friendship introductory phase. He had introduced her to all of his friends and included her
in many weekend plans. It was 3 months into
the relationship that it occurred to him: he had
never met her friends.

Every time he asked to hang out and she
was with her friends she had an excuse as to
why he couldn't come. Once, he vented, she
was sick and had her friends over for a sleep-
over. He offered to drop off soup and a movie
before heading to work – her favorite cold remedy - and she declined! Another time, he had
just come back into town after a family vacation
and when he called her to finalize their plans
for the evening she said she had a birthday
party to attend. He casually hinted at tagging
along (since he knew the birthday girl) and she
responded with, "I don't think that's such a
good idea."

Months after the break up, he wrote me
with an update. "I ran into a few of her friends
through a mutual friend. Turns out no one even
knew we were together! "

Now, this doesn't mean you'll be branded the awk-
ward cousin if you're not introduced to every friend and
invited to every social gathering. But it is worth noting
that there is a difference between not being invited to
things because 'friend time' is needed, and not being invited because you're being kept a secret.

Best-case scenario: your new lover is into some weird
shit he or she isn't comfortable sharing with you just yet.
Worst-case scenario, you're embarrassing to be with in

public, you're better kept a secret, or there's probably someone else. Regardless, you'll never know unless you bring it up. Mention that you respect having separate lives but would like to get to know his or her world as well.

Reality Slap: Although there are many people in relationships who pleasantly live separate lives, *most* people find a happy medium. Assuming you're not an embarrassing drunk and don't have a problem socializing with others, there's no reason why you shouldn't be invited to a birthday party –especially one where you know the birthday girl. If, for whatever reason, you're being left out of the loop it may be because you're not welcome. No matter the reason, the exclusion hurts. If you're vocal about it and still get turned down, it may be time to reevaluate the situation.

Insulting You to Others

Many would consider this a no brainer: bad-mouthing your partner has no place in a healthy relationship. So why does it happen?

Amanda* is a very good friend of mine who had been dating Rich* for about 6 months. One night, Rich had some friends over and didn't know Amanda had gotten off work early. She parked in the back and tip toed through the side door with Chinese take out in her hand. She could hear him talking but assumed he was on the phone. Once inside the kitchen, his murmurs turned into words and she heard him saying, "I mean she's just a little too emotional for my liking. She's either crying or going crazy." Amanda held her breath and crept closer to the living room, hiding in the darkness of the hallway. "Then why are you with her?" asked a recognizable male voice. "Dude, she's a wild ride in bed" was the response.

Amanda confronted Rich and he swore he had been trying to 'look cool' in front of his friends. She believed him and eventually forgave him.

About a month later, she received an email from a girl Rich knew. She claimed he had been trying to sleep with her. She swore nothing had happened but wanted Amanda to know the kind of person she was with; she included copies of Facebook messages they shared. They mainly consisted of him selling himself as today's Casanova. But as Amanda scrolled down, she found something that hurt her even more. "That crazy bitch? Nah. It's over. I'm trying to end it gently but who knows what she'll do. She loves me too much. I'm over it."

Insults don't always have to get to that level. Sometimes, they're miniscule things that just make you feel unappreciated and unsupported. We all have our embarrassing quirks; some we share privately with our lovers and assume they'll be kept a secret. Finding out your lover and his or her friends had a laugh fest about your Irritable Bowl Syndrome counts just as much as being called a crazy, emotional bitch.

If you catch this happening, you've got a right to walk away. There's nothing your partner could say that would justify him or her saying such bad things about you. If you've been blessed with the irresistible need to give others a second chance, do so at your own discretion. Words like that are never spoken without ill intent, and they're hardly ever a one-time deal.

Reality Slap: Making a good impression on your partner's friends is a hard enough without having to prove you're not a psychotic emotional wreck. You shouldn't have to worry about Todd knowing that anything dairy sends you to the bathroom in sweats. And although we all love to bitch and rant to our friends about how our significant other snores in bed, the line has to be drawn somewhere. If your partner noticeably puts you down to his or her posse, it shows there's no respect for your relationship. If he or she doesn't respect it, how is anyone else supposed to?

Insulting You to You

Yet another no brainer: It's a known fact that when you're in a relationship you've got to find 'nicer' ways to share your opinions. For example, you don't tell your girlfriend she's fat and has let herself go, you say, "I can barely tell the difference. It'll take you no time at all to get back to where you were." And then you suggest you sign up for a gym TOGETHER because you've been meaning to get into shape too. Right? *Right.*

Unfortunately, not everyone acknowledges the 'nicer' rule. In fact, there are people who thrive on making others feel inferior. And for some reason, there are people who put up with it. Mean things don't have to be delivered at a loud volume, nor do they have to be expressed during a fight. Real assholes insult their partners with sweet tones, over dinner, while being told about a recent promotion.

I remember getting ready for a party at a girlfriend's house. Her boyfriend was in the living room watching a football game. When we were ready to leave, we walked out and she did one of those cute runway walks that silently screamed, "How do I look?" He paused the game and looked over, barely able to hold in laughter – which was already repulsively insulting. Once he composed himself, he said, "Uh, you look *fine*. I doubt they'll even let you in though." And he burst into laughter. He didn't bother going into what was wrong with her outfit, he just enjoyed bringing her confidence down a few notches – in case she got tempted to chat up another guy. Needless to say, she walked around with a hunchback all night and barely made eye contact with anyone but me.

Insults come in different forms. The goal is to make you feel inferior so that he or she retains the power. It is done to make you feel like you can do no better than the person you're with and that if you try to leave, no one will accept you. The ability to arise fear or sadness in someone gives a person a false, yet addictive, sense of power.

On the off chance your partner doesn't know he or she is hurting your feelings, it doesn't hurt to speak up. However, make sure to do so firmly once, and nothing more. Any misunderstanding should be cleared up with you expressing how it hurts you. If it's not cleared up, it's not a misunderstanding; your partner is completely aware of the pain he or she is inflicting on you.

Reality Slap: If someone who claims to love you has the ability to make you cry and not be affected by it, you need to choose someone else. If you don't, you're signing up for a life of irreversible abuse. The relationship, as it stands now, is not about *you*; it's about the power you are giving your partner by allowing the cruelty to continue.

Public Embarrassment

This section could be summed up as a combination of the previous two: insulting you to others and insulting you to your face. Whatever the issues are at home, a couple is expected to practice a kind of decorum when in public. Such decorum entails avoiding verbal fights, insults and physical abuse. *Note: This does NOT mean fights- verbal or physical- are okay to do in private.* Yet how many times have you seen a guy grab a girl by the arm to remove her from a situation? How many times have you seen a woman yell at her man and call him names? Those people standing by will inevitably stop what they're doing, turn to look at what's going on and think, *Oh my. If that were to happen to me, I'd just die.*

I received an email from a male reader asking for relationship advice. His question was completely unrelated, but when filling me in on the details of his relationship, he mentioned an incident that occurred at a friend's graduation party that I could *not* shake off.

The girl he was dating was a shady character, leading him on while waiting for her 'dream guy' to become available. One night, they were all at a friend's graduation party and the girl made a move on her 'dream guy' while the male reader was in the bathroom. Well, turns out 'dream guy' wasn't interested and it sent the girl into a furious cycle. When male reader approached her for a public kiss, she lost it and screamed, "Ew! Get off!" He brushed it off and as she increasingly got more agitated, she suggested they'd leave. On the way out, he tried whispering that he'd make her feel better back at his place and she responded with, "With what? THAT THING?

When I refer to being in public, I don't only mean malls and parking lots; parties and intimate dinners count as well. The spotlight is on you and you're left to defend yourself while all the while dealing with the fact everyone around you is judging you. And if you're being insulted and embarrassed in public, chances are it's no better at home. Speaking up is crucial. People are quick to judge and not only do you not deserve to be made a fool, but you also don't want to be branded one by those around you; no one will respect you, they'll just feel bad for you.

Reality Slap: If your partner brushes you off and tells you you're overreacting, walk away. If someone has the ability to hurt you, is made aware of it and doesn't change his or her behavior, it's not someone who appreciates you or deserves you. All insults -public, private, or made behind your back- warrant a discussion. These are never to be ignored. It's important to present stability to those around you as well as to practice it at home. Anything less is just another reason to walk away.

Manipulation

Relationships are about compromise and sacrifice. Both parties do their part at pleasing one another and everyone, technically, ends up happy. The moment one becomes a slave to the other is when something is wrong. Although manipulation presents itself in many shapes and sizes, it's at its deadliest in the form of a guilt trip. Guilt trips can be used to get whatever the abuser desires, making you weak and helpless.

Dear Chiara,

Adam* and I have been together for 3 years and I'm stuck. I no longer see my friends and find myself going straight home from work every Friday. When we started dating, he was *all* about my friends and worked hard to win them over. But once we moved in together, happy hour Friday's became a thing of the past. It began with him telling me he didn't see me enough. I figured canceling on a few drink dates with the girls wouldn't be a big deal. But then he started making me feel guilty about going out without him. He'd say things like, "Well, I was planning on cooking you dinner and watching that movie you like but I guess I can just order in tonight. Go. Have fun."

I have no idea how it happened but I haven't seen my friends in months! I love him and want to be with him and I don't want him to think I'm choosing them over him. HELP!

Does this sound like you? If you're unsure but have a

feeling in your gut, try asking yourself the following questions:

• Do you feel like you're constantly giving, and never getting back?
• Do you find yourself doing things in the name of love that you would otherwise shun?
• Do you find yourself in situations that benefit your partner and hurt you?
• Do you feel inexplicably drained and exhausted?

There is no incentive for the manipulator to stop manipulating. It's up to you to stand up for yourself and make the demand. If your partner plays dumb and denies any wrongdoing, try making them understand how things make you feel. For instance, the girl from the email might want to say something like, "While you may not be doing this on purpose, I need you to know how much my friends mean to me and how much it hurts that you're making me choose." It's not always going to work, but the attempt is worth a shot. If you get no reaction, run.

Reality Slap: Depending on the degree of manipulation, you might be able to stop it in its tracks before it becomes a habit. However, if you find that cutting off one head grows three more, you may just be dealing with a born manipulator and you'll be better off cutting off ties. Catering one's life to someone else's can get *extremely* exhausting, not to mention it can leave you feeling lonely and unappreciated. There's a reason it takes the effort of two people to make a relationship successful; it's hard work.

The Stranger in Your Bed

During the first week of my first waitressing job, I met a very wise man in his early 40s. In the short weeks I knew him, he fed me little nuggets of wisdom I will never forget. One such nugget was the following: "It takes about a year or so into a relationship to see your partner's true colors. Everything before that is an elaborate charade." If I remembered his name, I would write him a thank you on behalf of every person I shared those words with, including myself.

You'd like to believe you know your significant other so well you could predict his or her every move. *You are so wrong*. If that were the case, affairs and secret fetishes would hardly shake anyone up. And while your partner may not be living the double life of a spy, it doesn't mean you know everything there is to know. It takes time to get to know someone; little quirks and stances on social issues aren't always discussed in your first 5 dates. The process of getting to know each other also becomes a lot harder if one of the parties refuses to cooperate.

I knew a guy, Steve*, whose brother was gay. The two were really close.

Steve met Ally* and the two of them immediately hit it off. Still, despite the magnetic attraction, he made it very clear that in order to be with him, Ally would have to be comfortable around homosexuals. She not only agreed but also gave him a speech on how supportive she was of gay rights and their right to marry. They started dating exclusively.

After about 11 months together, Steve's brother got serious with another man and brought him home for Thanksgiving dinner. Every time the couple shared a moment of affection, Ally was unable to hide her disgust and in a discussion on gay marriage, she made it clear that she didn't consider it valid in the eyes of God. This took Steve by complete surprise and he dumped her soon after.

The beginning phases of a relationship are often filled with sales pitches. You withhold information that may lower the chances of bagging a new mate; you sugarcoat your past and get creative about your future. We all do it so it's nothing to be ashamed of. But as the relationship progresses, you're expected to clear some of that up because, believe me, lies *will* come back to haunt you, and when they do, they're very likely to kick-flip perfection upside down.

Everyone is entitled to have secrets. As long as they don't hurt anyone, they're harmless. If, however, you feel like your partner is withholding something that could possibly wreak havoc on your relationship, you need to speak up. Sleeping next to someone you feel you don't know should be left to the experience of a one-night stand. If you encounter the same unfamiliarity in your relationship, something needs to be done.

Reality Slap: While it's important to respect your partner's privacy, it's also worth noting that being purposely kept in the dark can be extremely hurtful, not to mention possibly detrimental to your relationship. Maybe there's a reason your partner's not sharing his or her past. And if so much of it is hidden away, what other lies are you being told? You're entitled to know the person lying in your bed.

Addicted to the Pain. Why?

If any of your friends were dealing with someone who treated them this way, you'd have something to say about it. So the question is, why are *you* sticking around? Below are 5 common reasons

1. The good times are great
2. You're used to it and don't believe you deserve any better
3. You're certain things will change
4. You convince yourself that your partner can't possibly mean you harm
5. Your partner holds you hostage - emotionally

The Good Times Are Great:

We have a tendency to ignore shitty behavior when we have good memories to rely on. He calls you a whore in front of all your friends? No biggie. Remember the time he flew an airplane over your house that said, "I love you, Happy Anniversary"?

You're Used to It:

If you're someone who dates the same type of person over and over again, you're likely to be desensitized to the pain. In fact, you've become so used it that you can't imagine relationships being any different.

You're Certain Things Will Change:

Love often makes us see the best in people and as long as they express a desire to change, we're willing to invest everything we've got to see it happen – because we're certain it will. Once they catch on to the hope in your eyes, 'I'm trying to change' will become their go-to phrase every time they fuck up. These fuckers are ruthless.

You're Convinced Your Lover Couldn't Possibly Cause You Harm:

It's hard to admit that the person you love is consciously inflicting pain on you. And it's even harder to admit that you'd ever love anyone like that to begin with. So what do you do with things you can't make sense of? You convince yourself that nothing is going on; denial at its finest.

Your Partner Holds You Hostage — Emotionally:

Anytime you realize you're in a shitty situation and that you should get out, your partner rushes in with apologies, promises and more guilt trips, chaining you down just a little bit tighter. Love makes us vulnerable and in turn, we share our inner most weaknesses with the ones we love. Abusers take those weaknesses and use them to their advantages.

Knowing What You Deserve and Getting Out

There comes a point that you have to stop justifying your partner's behavior and realize that you're worth more than the abuse. There's no such thing as a perfect relationship, but if there were one, nothing listed in this chapter would be a part of it.

There are times that communication will do the trick. Once you mention the problem and it remains unresolved, you need to walk away. The toughest part is being able to call it quits.

Do this:

Take a pen and paper and jot down your idea of a healthy relationship. Write down everything you can think of – even the smallest details. Here are a few things to get you started:

1. How much freedom would you like to have?
2. Would you be allowed to see friends and family whenever you want?
3. How often would you have sex?
4. How would your partner respond to you getting fired?
5. What's your idea of a perfect Friday night together?
6. What would holidays be like together?
7. How much of your partner's past would you like to know?
8. How much of your lives would you share with one another?
9. How important are your partner's social skills?
10. What would your partner say about your friends?

11. What would your partner say about your style?
12. Would your partner support you when making life-changing decisions?

There are many more issues to address but the point isn't to make a checklist; it's for you to realize the things that matter to you sometimes become foggy when you fall in love. Compare your 'ideal' responses to the way things are in your current relationship and you'll see a difference between the two immediately.

Beware: There's a chance your partner isn't going to let you walk away easily. For people that enjoy hurting others, taking away that pleasure without their permission tends to rub them the wrong way. Your partner may lie and tell you what you want to hear in order to get you to stay; your partner may insult you, embarrass you or do everything in his or her power to ruin your good name. But you're stronger than their games and you're going to be just fine. (Make sure to check out the breaking up chapter at the end of the book.)

A relationship is like a puzzle; if even one piece is lost it'll never be complete. Get your ass to the store and buy yourself a new one.

6. The Leech

Many ingredients go into baking a healthy relationship. You need to be able to compromise and make sacrifices, and you need to support one another through thick and thin. When you give, you receive. In a healthy relationship there is a constant flow of give and take that leaves you feeling energized and never malnourished. *So why the hell are you so exhausted?*

There's a reality we choose to ignore when dealing with unhealthy relationships: they are inexplicably draining on our psyches. Do you ever feel like no matter how hard you try you can never get your head above water? You're sure you're doing all of the right things yet the relationship seems to be going backwards and you don't know why. The answer is simple: someone who claims to love you is sucking the living life out of you.

There are two types of leeches: the **physical leech** and the **emotional leech**. The physical leech is your typical gold-digging, low life who takes physical things from you. This can include anything from actual cash to the roof over your head. The emotional leech, on the other hand, takes everything else from you including your sanity, your independence, your optimism and more.

The Physical Leech

The **physical leech** is one who takes things you work for and gives nothing of value in return. He or she may be blunt about using you or may feed you lies and empty promises in exchange for the material goods.

The Gold Digger

In the past, the term used to refer solely to women attaching themselves to the rich man's ball sack in order to obtain material things – i.e. cars, rent, new expensive clothes, etc. Today's world, however, has witnessed a rise in the number of successful women as well, creating a market for the younger male to latch on to.

There's no shame in the game, you've got the money and the gold digger wants it. This is all fine and dandy if you're a trust fund baby who only cares for arm candy. But for those who work hard for their income and/or crave a real connection, having to constantly question whether they're wanted for money can prove to be an annoying and draining task.

Your partner should never *ask* you to buy them something and if they do it better be once in a blue moon. Watch out for tricksters shuffling through their pockets when the bill finally arrives. Give her time to *really* find her wallet while she absent-mindedly shuffles through her purse. Now, don't get me wrong, treating one another is important in a relationship. What I'm referring to is the repeat offender, not an ounce of guilt while watching your wallet rapidly shrink.

The I-swear-I'm-looking-for-a-job

In today's economy, it's almost a believable excuse. The person you may have started dating with the hot-shot job may have been let go due to budget cuts; how are you supposed to, in good conscience, give someone shit for that? We seldom question the efforts of those we love, especially when we fear an unfavorable outcome.

Consequently, combining the current state of the economy and the blindfold love puts snuggly over your eyes, it's easy to assume your partner is doing everything in his or her power to get a job when really, it's simply a matter of being a lazy fuck.

If someone felt their life was at stake, you better believe that the second they lost their job, they'd be hitting the pavement to find another. Desperate times call for desperate measures, right? PhD's are suddenly serving you food at your local pizza joint; executives are suddenly mowing your lawn. Why? Because you do whatever it takes to get food in your mouth and to keep up with the rent.

That sense of urgency and desperation for survival disappears when you're unemployed and there is still food on the table and a roof over your head, Now, don't get me wrong, there are people who would hit the pavement regardless of their partner's financial standing, as a statement of independence. But for those who lack that inner drive, it's always easier to strip down to your panties and turn on your favorite TV show instead of heading to Kinko's to print out your resume.

The Low Life

This is the partner who doesn't bother making promises. The low life eats your food, crashes on your couch after a night of partying and bones you in the morning. Class at its finest. And you allow it.

Those who fall victim to the low life's charm are people who are in dire need of company and would rather be fooled into thinking someone cares for them over having to admit they're being used. If you're one of these people, you're probably shaking your head saying, "I can take away my house key any time I want!"

There isn't much hope for this scenario. Leeching of this kind is done consciously and often without an ounce of guilt. So while you're slaving away at your two jobs, your lover is at home making a mess he or she expects you to clean up. Because in the end, *the leech* is doing you the favor by loving you, right? Who else would love someone like you? Surely, not someone with any self respect. Right?

♥

You're clearly not getting anything of value in return. Everything you've worked for is being taken from you in exchange for the illusion of love. How does that make you feel? Those long hours you spend at work to make ends meet mean nothing when your 'lover' is the one reaping the benefits. Where does that leave you? In today's world, both parties contribute financially. If you think this behavior will stop once the two of you get married, you've got another thing coming.

If you're not walking away, one of two things is going on: either you accepted the fact you've become an enslaved doormat to your partner or you've realize the absurdity but feel too guilty to leave, knowing very well that someone you care for has become completely reliant on you. Either way, you're fucked. The sooner you put your foot down, the easier it will be to reclaim your dignity.

The Emotional Leech

Emotional leeching is more common than physical. It is also a lot more discrete. When you fall in love with someone, the walls you've worked so hard to build crumble down in weakness, leaving you exposed. And unfortunately, there are many people out there willing to exploit your vulnerability for their gain.

While the physical leech leaves you with an empty wallet, the **emotional leech** leaves you with en empty soul. Relationships shouldn't be exhausting, yet so many are. That's why so many people are turned off by the idea of commitment. Let's take a look at some common emotional bloodsuckers, shall we?

The Clingy and Possessive

Does having to report your every move, having a curfew, and not being allowed to see a certain group of friends sound familiar? Sure. It should remind you of your teenage years – not your adult ones. If you happen to get the two mixed up, take a look below for a few signs to look out for:

1. Over contact: An overabundance of texts, calls, Facebook posts, emails and tweets
2. Intense jealousy: Puts a question mark around every person you're friends with, male or female

3. There are rules: Who you're allowed to see, when and where
4. Dictatorship: Regarding all aspects of your life – social, financial, etc.
5. Joint lives: You're not allowed to have a life outside of the relationship

In a healthy relationship, you should be able to share your lives freely at your discretion; no threats and demands necessary. It's easy to believe the points listed above are a part of every relationship, but they're not. And when such things are demanded of us, the relationship becomes a chore –a draining, exhausting chore.

Take a look at Appendix D and Appendix E for signs you're dating a possessive cling machine.

The One With the Extra Baggage

Relationships take a lot of work. No matter how they turn out, a little bit of every relationship stays with you – as it's meant to. But there are limits. Something all too common is the person who, for whatever reason, can't let go. Whether it's the past itself, or the insecurities that have resulted from it, dealing with these types of people can get remarkably exhausting – no matter how in love you think you may be.

For being the one without the baggage, you have to do a shit ton of work. You constantly have to reassure your significant other that you're not like his or her ex. You have to adhere to specific rules and tiptoe around issues to ensure your partner doesn't turn into a psycho. You have to constantly deal with irrational fears and if you know anything about irrational fears, you know you can't use logic to calm them. Before you know it, your day is over before it begins.

This type of emotional leech is hard to deal with because on paper, they don't seem like they are doing anything wrong. In most cases, the past is revealed way before things get serious in the new relationship, and technically, you know exactly what you're walking into. Unfortunately, the moment you realize the person you're with hasn't gained closure or grown from their past it will be too late; you'll be in too deep and you'll experience serious guilt for even considering leaving.

The Demanding Nag

This type of leech is under the impression that a relationship should parallel a dictatorship. While it is true that certain aspects of your lives are expected to merge as you become exclusive, it doesn't mean one becomes a slave to the other.

At first, it's something you and your friends joke about. "Yeah, I do it just to keep her happy so she leaves me alone!" And then one day, you wake up and realize you've lost all control over your life and have become a slave to catering to the needs and wants of the demanding individual you're supposed to 'love'. You get used to the sighs and the eye rolls and the late night phone calls, wondering where you are. Just remember, you moved out of your parents' house for a reason.

The Energy Drain

A positive outlook and an overall excitement for life is one of the most irresistible qualities anyone could share. Imagine having everything in common with someone, except that. When you want to go out for a drink, your partner wants to stay in. When you want to go on an adventure, your partner presents you with a list of reasons not to. And then one day, you shoot yourself in the face.

Imagine the lover who is always pessimistic. Imagine having to come home to someone who is in a constant sour attitude, even when you want to announce your job promotion. Or how about the person who hates public outings and embarrasses you with their lack of effort at your best friend's birthday party? You feel like you're always dragging them by the ear and offering an ice cream cone if they participate. This can get really fucking exhausting.

This is another hurdle often masked by romance. Some people get 'tired' after years of living life and decide to take a breather. If you're not as worn out, it's going to affect your relationship. And if having similar lifestyles wasn't one of the things that drew the two of you together in the first place, this is something you're likely to encounter. Because regardless of whether or not you're in a relationship, you're bound to get that hunger to go live life. If you're not ready to be a depressed homebody hermit, no amount of love is going to make you.

♥

A lot of these scenarios go by unnoticed because they aren't physical. It happens when you aren't even looking; you suddenly wake up one morning and realize you've never felt so tired and you can't explain why. Yet you know something isn't right. Not having the evidence to hold in your hand, you figure your reasons for speaking up aren't valid.

Knowing What Matters

At the beginning of the book, we talked about knowing what is worth sacrificing in the name of love.

1. Independence
2. Everything you've earned
3. Sanity
4. Emotional well being
5. Individuality
6. Social life
7. Optimism
8. Strength
9. Privacy
10. Happiness

Never give those up.

Relationships are hard work but that hard work should come from both parties, not just one. You should never feel like a slave to your partner and you should always be willing to speak up when you do. There is a very big difference between being supportive and being a doormat; learn it and realize what you're worth.

Somewhere along the way, we've come to believe that love means catering to your partner's every need and desire. On paper, that sounds like a fairy tale come true. But in reality, you cannot possibly do so in a healthy manner without getting the same in return.

You are expected to suck the living life out of your partner when you need it and allow your partner to do it back when they need it. You are the strength today and the weakness tomorrow. Constantly feeding another entity without receiving anything in return is bound to leave you malnourished and that is exactly the opposite of what love is supposed to do.

You're likely to experience a lot of guilt in this type of a relationship. When you are someone's sole source of nutrients – be it financial or emotional – and are constantly feeding them, you inevitably begin to believe they'd die of poor nutrition without you. Almost like the annoying stray cat that stops by for dinner every night that you've come to love.

If you find yourself in this scenario, speak up. There are times the leech feeds without being conscious of it. And you're entitled to voicing how you feel. Approach the situation with the assumption that it *is not* being done on purpose and don't be combative. Make sure to lie out exactly how you feel and as always, flip the switch and ask your partner how he or she would feel if the roles were reversed. A light bulb should turn on somewhere. Remind yourself that you are entitled to being in a relationship that gives back as much as you put in.

If the leeching continues, cut them off. It doesn't matter how madly in love you think you may be, *this will suck you dry.* The longer you're with the person, the weaker you'll be the day you realize you need nutrients passed through an IV. No matter how great the times together, a relationship is meant to nourish *you* and make you a stronger and better person. If your partner is the only one powering up, it's time to do something about it.

7. The Physical Abuser

Chapter 5 focused on verbal abuse and it was the longest chapter thus far. There's a reason: abuse comes in many, many forms. To categorize it into only two, verbal and physical, is barely scratching the surface. I'd like to make it clear that I am not a licensed psychologist and am in no way qualified to give professional advice – on any of the subjects of this book, really. I am, however, going to attempt approaching the topic nonetheless because I have experienced it first hand. Take it as friendly advice.

As with any other mirage, it most often comes out of nowhere. One day you're happy and smitten over your new lover and the next, you're curled up in the corner of the bedroom, scared, wishing time would stop. You find yourself in so deep; you don't know how to get out, even when your life depends on it. Let's approach this mirage delicately, beginning with my own story.

My Story

Believe it or not, I have dated *almost* every mirage

listed in this book. I haven't felt the need to share my
personal stories because they're just like yours. This relationship, however, continues to haunt me – even 10
years later. It is hearing about others and their encoun-
ters with abuse that has played a huge role in my emotional recovery. We will call him Mike.

I met Mike through a mutual friend. He represented
all the rebellion I wish I had stood for at the time. I en-
vied his anarchist attitude and his love for *terrible* under-
ground punk music. I was going through my years of
rebellion and decided I wanted him to lead the way. Besides, he was 4 years older and he seemed to know what
he was doing.

Dating an older guy – and remember, when you're
young, a 4 year age gap translates into a 10 year gap-
was exhilarating. At that point, I had already lost my
virginity and discovered what I believed to be my sexu-
ality. We began having sex, and for the first month of our
relationship, I was on Cloud 9. Then, the winds began to
change.

He opened up about his family drama – mommy and
daddy didn't love him very much – and his father's constant neglect. He started spending all of his time at my
house and I became his go-to confession helpline for everything fucked up going on in his mind. This was a
heavy burden for a little girl to bear.

Since all of my free time went to him, I had little to
no interaction with my friends other than lunch breaks at
school. When it came to Friday night, he'd beg me to ac-
company him to see his friends; more than beg, he'd
guilt trip me. Before I knew it, my friends had slipped
through my fingers. At first, I blamed the lack of contact
on them and found solace in the fact my boyfriend was
always there to listen. I genuinely believed they had de-
serted me.

Eventually, however, everything came crumbling down. I couldn't make sense of it at the time but looking back, I realize I was just no longer interested in being with him. The isolation had gotten to me. (That's why I'm so adamant about keeping friends in your life no matter your relationship status.) In addition to the isolation, his weaknesses were beginning to bother me as well and I no longer felt that physical, bad boy attraction I had once swooned over. The sex became a chore and after a few weeks, I avoided it all together. He wasn't a fan of my decision.

On Halloween of that year, a couple of my friends were attending the Santa Monica Parade. This is one of Los Angeles's biggest events and I had never seen it. I asked Mike to come *weeks* ahead of time, securing my ride. I was so excited to see my friends I could hardly contain myself.

While stuck in LA traffic, the topic of sex, or the lack-there-of, came up. "Why won't you have sex with me anymore?" he asked. "You're never in the mood when I try to touch you. You always pull away like I disgust you." I remember this conversation vividly. It was the beginning of the end.

"I'm just not in the mood. I'm sorry" I responded, looking awkwardly onto the red lights ahead. "Well WHAT THE FUCK!" he suddenly screamed. "I *DE-SERVE* sex. Look at everything I do for you!" His breaths were getting deeper and I began trying to diffuse the situation by suggesting we talk about it after the parade. *Yeah, nice try.*

He grabbed the wheel and turned onto a small side street. "We're not fucking going to see your friends. What do you think; I'll just drive you everywhere without you fucking me? I *DESERVE* to be fucked." I didn't respond. "TALK TO ME!" he yelled. I decided that anything that would come out of my mouth would infuriate him further and because he was behind the wheel, he had my life in his hands. I considered telling him what he wanted to hear but my pride overrode any common sense. "TALK TO ME!" he repeated, now louder than ever before. I started crying and asked him to stop the car. *Nice. Try.*

At this point, he started screaming so loudly that he began to cry. Then, suddenly, he yelled, "IF YOU CAN'T FUCKING TALK TO ME, YOU CAN'T FUCKING TALK TO ANYONE YOU STUPID BITCH!" He stepped on the accelerator, put his head against the steering wheel and headed straight for the car in front of us. I launched my body against his to take control of the wheel and was able to stop the collision.

The rest of the night is a blur. He dropped me off and came inside, crying uncontrollably. I held *him* in my bed as he apologized for everything that had happened. I told him I accepted his apology and asked that he never scare me like that again. That night, he begged me to sleep with him. I did.

That night he raped me. Although I had agreed to the sex, in the middle of the session he began getting rough. I screamed, "STOP" and he didn't. He didn't acknowledge it. I said it again and again and nothing changed. He only went harder. I buried my face in the pillow and cried, leaving my body and never fully getting it back. Once he finished, he asked me what was wrong. I told him I had asked him to stop because it hurt and he responded, "Oh. I didn't hear you."

Those words continue to haunt me today.

The following week, I joined an afterschool program and met another guy. This guy was everything Mike was not and we began, discretely, talking online. Mike found out and I just happened to be sitting on his lap when he saw the new guy's message pop up on the computer screen. He grabbed me and pushed me against the wall. That day, I decided to leave him.

It didn't go well. I had to lock my doors and keep 911 on speed dial. I couldn't pick up my phone because he blocked his number and called from payphones. Looking back, a restraining order was absolutely necessary but what the hell does a little girl know about restraining orders?

The relationship didn't last long but it affects my life every day. I've always spoken openly about it but it's far from being dealt with. I felt like I was being held captive in my own life, with no way out. Still, deep within, I felt the instinct to survive and knew I had to escape. Physical abuse is one of the most life altering experiences an individual can go through. Ten years later, I am just now dealing with what was left unresolved.

What is Physical Abuse?

Below are just 5 things to look out for. For further reading, please refer to the resources provided at the end of this chapter.

1. Your partner strikes you, causes you physical pain – either directly or with a foreign object
2. You partner exhibits aggressive behavior with objects or people surrounding you to scare you
3. Your partner puts you in physical danger like, for example, leaving you in an unsafe environment
4. Your partner physically dictates your behavior like, for example, locking you in the car

5. Your partner sexually assaults you, rapes you or coerces you into engaging in sexual behavior

Abuse in general - be it verbal or physical - is a lot more common than you think. It doesn't have to resemble what you see on television; it doesn't have to leave you with visible bruises. You can be pinned against the wall for 30 seconds as he/she yells at you and be just as scarred as you would be if you were cut in the face with a blade. The varying degrees give room for a wide range of experiences. So many people suffer in silence and endure the abuse. And although verbal abuse can occur independent of the physical, the latter almost always occurs with the former.

The Discrete Transition

Not many of us would knowingly commit to an abusive relationship. You don't begin a first date by saying, "Hi. I'm Mike. I like to listen to music and my favorite color is red. I also enjoy manipulating my lovers with guilt and forcing myself on to them when they've made it clear they're not interested. Really hope you're interested in a second date!" If that were the case, the number of incidents of domestic abuse wouldn't be so high. The transition is *usually* a silent one.

It usually begins with verbal abuse. One way or another, the abuser finds a way to manipulate you and you lose most of your control – in the beginning. The physical acts tend to start small; we just don't notice them. What initially seems like an innocent tug towards the exit is actually a physical act of control, and you end up feeling like a child in trouble. These acts are so common you hardly ever notice them.

Rape and Other Sexual Assault

Sex is something that should be shared by two consenting adults. I know, it sounds cliché but believe me, there's a reason – other than the obvious- that I say that. It's easy to believe that sex is 'owed' in a relationship. *Poor chap, only getting it twice a month, why am I being so stingy?* The second you begin doing it for your partner and not because you want it, you're objectifying yourself. You may think you're doing it to shut your partner up and to keep him or her happy but your genitals aren't collectibles to be traded. This will make you feel used and the feeling will crawl up on you when you least expect it.

You should feel comfortable with *everything* you do in bed. If your partner gets too aggressive, you have to speak up. And remember that sex is not owed; no one has the right to come demand it of you – whether they physically force you or try to talk you into doing it.

You Don't Deserve It

The abuser will likely make you believe everything is your fault; that you deserve everything you are getting and that he or she has no other choice *but* to act that way. You may be told obedience is required or that sex is owed. The abuser may also use words to belittle you and to take away your strength. So where does that leave you? Feeling like utter worthless shit.

Anyone can tell you that you aren't worthless and that you don't deserve the abuse but it'll fly right over your head. Why? Because *you* don't believe it. The only hope for you is the fact that deep down inside, buried under all the pain, you KNOW you don't deserve this and you KNOW this is not your fault.

Imagine your closest friend and place him or her in your same scenario. What would you say if your friend believed she deserved to be punched in the face for forgetting to make dinner on time? I hardly doubt you'd agree, right? So what makes you think it's any different for you?

No one, no matter what the crime is, deserves to be hurt – physically or verbally. The pain is inflicted not because you deserve to feel it but because **the abuser feels the need to inflict it**. If he or she were dating anyone else, that person would get the same exact abusive treatment. So it is NOT your fault.

Getting Out

First and foremost, it's important to know that no matter how well you behave, the abuse will never end, your partner will never change, and things will never get better. The abuser will always find a reason to maintain control over you or those you care about. The relationship you're in will never be salvaged; you need to get out.

It's also important to know, in case you're in denial about the relationship, that *this is NOT love.* Love doesn't intentionally bruise or scar, it doesn't isolate you from friends and family and it does not make you believe you're a worthless piece of shit. Real love is supportive, kind, gentle and empowering. Don't let the illusion take over, no matter how badly you want it to be true. The person you are with doesn't love you.

Leaving an abusive partner is always easier said than

done; he will do everything in his power to keep you under his control – be it through threats or guilt. If you feel your safety is in danger, take a look at the resources at the end of this chapter and get help. Begin with a restraining order and look up shelters in your area.

Getting a Restraining Order

The process of obtaining a restraining order varies, depending on where you live. For general guidelines please visit:

http://stoprelationshipabuse.org/how-to-get-a-restraining-order/

In most cases, this can give you the peace of mind necessary to go on with your life. The process is generally quick and you will be given a temporary restraining order to carry with you until your court date. If safety is an issue, getting a restraining order is one of the first things you need to do.

RESOURCES

<u>United States</u>
The National Domestic Violence Hotline
http://www.thehotline.org/
(800) 799 – 7233 (SAFE)

Men:
The Domestic Abuse Helpline for Men and Women

http://dahmw.org
(888) 743 – 5754

UK
Women's Aid
http://www.womensaid.org.uk/
0808 2000 247

Men:
Mankind Initiative
http://mankind.org.uk
01823 334244

CANADA
The National Domestic Violence Hotline
http://www.thehotline.org/
(800) 363 – 9010

AUSTRALIA
The National Domestic Violence Hotline
http://dvrc.org.au/support-services/national-services/
(800) 200 - 526

Men:
One in Three Campaign
http://oneinthree.com.au

INTERNATIONAL
International Directory of Domestic Violence Agencies Worldwide
http://www.hotpeachpages.net
For shelters, hotlines, refuges and crisis centers

8. If It's Dead, Bury It

Love is an amazing feeling. When it flows through your veins at its highest velocity, you feel like you could conquer the world within the blink of an eye. It's one of the biggest highs in life, comparable to the best of drugs. So when it disappears, you're left with the miserable come down, begging for more, looking everywhere for that one last hit; and like any drug addict, you'll do whatever it takes to get it.

You have a hard time letting things go and leaving them in the past. You're so convinced that the universe has gotten *something* wrong that you're willing to ignore all of the red flags to prove it was meant to be. And as you bring out that Ouija board to perform the séance, you're completely oblivious to the fact you've become a foolish, delusional, crazy person.

This is one of the most common mirages and one of the saddest delusions. You so badly want to believe something isn't dead that you're willing to do whatever it takes to revive it, even if it means hurting yourself and the person you claim to love. You'd do anything to feel that high again, one last time, *wouldn't you?* This is exactly what this chapter is about: your inability to face rehab.

Unfortunately, no good can come of your, pathetic attempts. Being in denial will only make the fall harder to bear; you don't get landing pads during heartbreak. The first step is acknowledging the fact you're holding on to something with no heartbeat. Once you come to terms with reality, we can deal with moving on with your life.

Let's begin by scoping out a few common scenarios. Something below should ring a bell.

Common Scenarios

The Dreadful Label:

You should commit because of how you feel about one another, not the label you're under. This scenario is much too common. The moment you rely on the label to carry you through the hardships of a relationship is the moment your journey with denial begins. This is why hurrying to label a connection is pointless; without the feelings to back it up, it's just a title. Be careful not to chase your interpretation of a label; it'll always be subjective.

Reality Slap: Imagine the conversation. Your partner yells, "I don't love you anymore!" You respond, "But we're boyfriend and girlfriend!" Sounds a bit ridiculous, doesn't it? There isn't anything a title can do for you that real genuine feelings cannot: if it's over, it's over.

The only time a label should play any sort of role is if the couple is married. Whether you genuinely believe in the sanctity of marriage or you just want to avoid dealing with the chaos that is divorce, the relationship deserves a little extra effort. This is especially true if children are involved. Consider marriage counseling, it can do wonders for a broken home. Once the effort has been made, however, know when to accept the label as just another word in the dictionary.

History Says So:

Staying in an unhappy relationship and trying to make it work because of how long you've been together is a recipe for disaster. Every relationship has history, but the past doesn't guarantee a future. If you're with someone for 3 years, it's not enough reason to beat the relationship into the ground when feelings happen to fade. In fact, the longer you're with someone, the more likely they *are* to fade. So stop using the duration of your relationship as a reason to pretend hope exists.

Reality Slap: It doesn't matter how long you are with a person. In some cases, a three-month relationship can be better than a yearlong relationship. Do not make the mistake of relying on your past to get you through the hardships; the past is the reason the two of you stand where you stand today: broken.

Beating Stick:

Maybe you missed something. Maybe your partner didn't understand the last point you were trying to make and maybe it's worth repeating, for the fifth time. Maybe your boyfriend isn't quite clear on how amazing you look in red lingerie; you should try it again – just in case. And gentlemen, make sure to appeal to her soft side by making reservations at her favorite restaurant, ordering her favorite dish and then taking her on the same magic carpet ride you took her on when you first met – that'll remind her of the butterflies. Okay, if you're not seeing the desperation yet, you're a lost cause.

Reality Slap: Ladies, your boyfriend knows exactly what you look like in red lingerie and it stopped giving him a hard-on months ago. Adding crotch less panties isn't going to do it. And gentlemen, she might smile and find the gesture sweet but it's not going to have the same effect on her as it did the first time you went out. You will continue to believe that trying the same thing in different ways is what your relationship needs to be revived, when really all it needs is a little spunk.

Afraid of Letting Go:

One of two things is going on here: either you're holding on to the death of yesterday hoping it'll be revived today, or you're just scared of being alone. Waking up next to misery is better than waking up alone, right? *Wrong.* Go back to Chapter 1 if you need to and revisit the section on fearing solitude. Once you learn to depend on yourself for happiness rather than on somebody else, you'll see that being single really isn't that bad. You're not only depriving your partner of the potential for happiness but you're depriving yourself as well. Don't be afraid, there's a lot to experience out there.

Reality Slap: All this energy you're putting into your inability to detach is a complete and utter waste. It would be put to much better use accepting reality and opening your doors to something new. Stop being a coward; once you gain the confidence to take on the world alone, you'll become addicted to the high and reject everything but perfection.

The Lingering Period Post-Break Up:

There are very few relationships that *completely* end on command. Most relationships linger... pointlessly. It's kind of like the eyes that continue to blink after a person is beheaded. The lingering process is an interesting phenomenon, especially considering that most relationships consist of a dumper and a dumpee. So, you might ask, if at least one party wanted the relationship to end, how the hell can the relationship still linger?

Blame it on routine. You know the person; you don't have to deal with all that is scary about meeting someone new; it's guaranteed time between the sheets; and no matter the hardships, there is something irresistible about how close the past has brought you. But it's easy to mistake that closeness for romance and destiny. And when it comes to letting go of the old, trying something new can be a little scary.

Unfortunately, the lingering period hardly ever resembles the old relationship. When you leave your ex's house the morning after you meet for drinks to 'catch up', you might notice you don't feel quite as fulfilled, the sex was mediocre at best, and truthfully, you feel a bit used. *Right?*

Then come the late night "I'm lonely" phone calls, looking for comfort from the person that used to hand it out so freely. You just need that reassurance, you just want someone to love you and care about the shitty day you've had. You continue to look for something that no longer exists. Even if, out of weakness, the two of you break down and try again, the relationship will be short lived. *Why?* Because the lingering period is not the relationship you're pretending it is.

Reality Slap: The relationship ended for a reason. Somewhere deep within, one – or both of you- knew that it was over. But letting go of something you've known for so long can be a scary process, so you hide deep within the walls of denial and stick to what you know. As hard as it may be, however, you have to learn to believe that things happen for a reason. The lingering period only postpones the inevitable.

You've Broken Up and You're Still Holding On

All you can think about is how great the good times were; how amazing it felt to be in each other's arms; and how the world seemed to turn to the rhythm of your heartbeats. You can't help but believe those feelings will come rushing back in if you hold on just a little longer. You are addicted to hope, even when all of the signs tell you to run the opposite direction. We get it, letting go is hard to do.

What not being able to let go is REALLY doing to you

Having hope and faith is healthy and, generally, encouraged in life - we'd be a sad species without it. That's assuming, however, that you know when to give up. And if you're reading this chapter, you probably don't. Not only does putting all your eggs in one basket suck the living life out of you, but it also keeps you isolated from everything your life could potentially become if you allowed it to progress.

Not being able to let go sends you into a world of delusional thinking. You come to believe that the person is the *only* person for you and that if you don't make it work, you're destined to be alone forever. The prospect of finding a dream partner begins to fade and your life becomes about settling; it becomes about making lemonade out of the shitty lemons life hands you rather than going to the store and buying the brand you like. Dreams fade and you eventually believe that struggle is what love is all about. The past will haunt you and never let you move on and that's a shitty life for a broken heart, don't you think?

Having said that, sometimes obsessing is an important part of the process. If you absolutely *cannot* let go, go ahead and abuse the shit out of 'what used to be'. Really, it will help with the closure; you will just hit rock bottom and be in even more pain than you are now, but at least you will no longer be in denial. Sometimes it takes experiencing a lesson to really learn it. It's kind of like being a teenager, only you don't get grounded as punishment; you just get your heart broken, over and over again. Really, if you think this is what you need, go for it!

Okay, to be clear, I'm not promoting self-harm. The reality is, different people learn in different ways and every relationship is different. If you can't make sense of your relationship dying because your partner told you he or she loved you just a week before, maybe you need the door slammed in your face for clarification. Maybe you just need to be slapped a few times, regardless of your situation. *Who knows?* We will talk more about this in Chapter 12.

Stop what you're doing and walk away

You can beat the living shit out of your relationship; it will not come back to life. You're chasing something that isn't there and you'll soon run out of gas. Don't you think you deserve better? In this case, being resilient and not giving up is not an admirable trait - it doesn't make you a warrior of love. Just unroll your sleeves, put down the bat, and allow yourself to breathe.

If you were the one to end the relationship, consider the reasons you did so in the first place. Ask yourself, are the reasons it ended likely to come back? Have the issues *really* been resolved? Can you go back to the way things were without anything changing between you? Deep inside, when you ended it, you knew something was wrong and you began the process of letting go. You just got a little lost along the way.

If you were dumped, accept it. Romantic comedies lie; showing up at the airport as your ex is boarding a plane is not the grand romantic gesture that's going to rebuild a broken home. Your partner left you for a reason. You can go home and work on a power point presentation and try to sell the shit out of yourself and the reasons the relationship deserves a second shot, but you'll only be wasting your time. Accept it and stop obsessing. And remember the cliché: when one door closes, another door opens.

♥

Last Minute Tip: If you're still in the relationship, try mentally stepping out of it and observing it objectively. Look at all of the signs and make the executive decision to walk away and leave it for what it used to be. Know that by beating it to the ground, you risk mutilating your relationship beyond recognition. The good times will be harder to remember, too.

A Note

Although rare, there are times in a relationship when the flame goes out for a bit and just needs a little gas. But beware; there is a big difference between this and everything we just covered. If you can relate to anything in this chapter, deep down inside, you know the relationship is over. Your attempts are out of desperation and fear, and you're telling yourself what you need to hear in order to be happy. When a flame needs to be relit, however, both parties know there's still enough wax to sustain the wick. In your case, you're seeing a candle that has burned into oblivion.

Sometimes, people just need a break and it doesn't mean the relationship is over forever; the universe is just telling you right now isn't the right time. You have to listen and respond accordingly. If your relationship is falling apart, it may be because one party needs to deal with outside factors before being able to fully commit. And if that's the case, your partner deserves that chance. Otherwise, your relationship will never reach its full potential.

Sometimes, breaking up is a mistake, yes. But don't be fooled into thinking you're equipped to make that call. If the two of you are meant to be together and there is something left worth fighting for, it'll present itself when it's ready.

Make sure you know which scenario you're in and be honest with yourself. You're not doing any one a favor by lying; you're only prolonging the inevitable.

9. Commitment Phobe

You're not the first to face this utterly shitty situation. You meet someone who excites every fiber of your being only to be brutally rejected by the words, "I'm not looking for anything 'serious.'" The world around you spins in confusion as you go over how magnificent things are between the two of you. *This doesn't make any sense! Things seemed to be going so well, is it me??*

Although this chapter tackles different types of issues with commitment, it's worth noting that commitment phobia really does exist. A phobia is a type of anxiety disorder. Those who suffer from this particular one often encounter problems committing to other aspects of their lives as well, including all things social and career related; the phobia doesn't only apply to romantic commitments.

There are a couple of other things worth noting. First of all, although it's *usually* men who experience issues with commitment, women can be just as guilty - such issues know no gender. It's important to avoid making assumptions and to not use the gender card when making accusations. And secondly, although commitment phobia is real, remember there is always a possibility that you're simply getting used; your new lover may just want to have their cake and eat it too. Unfortunately, this is usually the case.

Why is this considered a mirage?

You will often do whatever it takes to keep someone you care about around – regardless of the kind of pain the relationship (or in this case, lack-there-of) inflicts on you. Sounds like every other mirage in this book, right? You will put your life and everything you want from it on hold in hopes that one day the object of your affection will be ready to be with you. If you believe that's all it takes to make someone want to commit to you, you've come face to face with a mirage.

Why would someone have issues with commitment?

Before we dive in, let's consider why issues with commitment exist in the first place. Later in the chapter, we're going to take a look at the different types of offenders. It may not be as simple as connecting Point A to Point B, but considering the complexities of the human experience might help you understand what you're up against.

1. A troubled upbringing

The first thing to affect the lifestyle of an individual is the way in which they were raised. If, for example, there was infidelity or divorce in the home it may alter the individual's perception of commitment in his/her own future.

2. A bitch of an ex

We've all had our hearts broken, shattered and

mercilessly spat back out at us. Most of us survive –eventually – while others let the pain affect their every future move. This can easily repel someone from wanting to commit again.

3. A necessary part of the growing process

Sometimes you get into something serious before you're ready and when it comes crumbling down, you find yourself craving freedom and the need to experience other options. Jumping into something too soon is a sure way to turn someone off from future commitments.

4. Overall lack of interest

There are people out there who couldn't give two shits about romance. All they care for is the physical/sexual reward and their main focus remains on other parts of their lives – for example: career, friends and family.

5. A high for the chase

Sometimes it has nothing to do with you or what the two of you may or may not share. Sometimes, it's all about the chase. The courtship phase of a relationship is always the most exciting – texts, emails, flirting, teasing and experimentation. Once the prize is won, what's the use in sticking around? It's time for the next challenge, of course.

♥

The above are just five possibilities that could explain issues with commitment. Remember that no two scenarios are alike. In fact, it can even be a *combination* of reasons, not just one. In other words, it's important never to assume when it comes to interpreting your partner's behavior. You may point fingers and accuse your lover of being a player unable to commit when really, he's simply scared shitless of ending up like his parents. Don't jump the gun, Sherlock.

Warning Signs

Now that we know a few reasons commitment issues exist, let's dive into a few red flags you should keep an eye out for. If you're reading this chapter, it's likely that you've either been told commitment was an issue or that you just have a gut feeling something wasn't right. Regardless, it's important to consider how each warning sign could cause trouble in your potential relationship.

The Dating Track Record

How many serious relationships has the person in question been in? Taking a peek into the past might help you get an idea of who you're dealing with. If all you see is a bunch of hit-it and quit-its, you may want to approach with caution.

Courtship – Full speed ahead

Watch out. Those who fear or purposefully avoid commitment have absolutely no problem going full force through the dating phase. This can easily emulate perfection; they know they'll never commit so they'll do what it takes to get their needs met. Making you fall head over heels is part of the game.

Nothing friend, family or work related — for either of you

Whatever the excuse is, you haven't been able to introduce your new lover to anyone you know; everyone is starting to believe the whole fling is a figment of your imagination. *What gives?* Introducing someone new to people in your world is the next step towards permanence. Once the introduction has been made, people are bound to assume a relationship is, or will soon be, in full effect. Those with commitment issues don't want anyone assuming anything of that sort so they steer clear of any dangerous events – i.e. birthdays, holiday dinners, company banquets, etc.

Everything last minute

If dealing with a real commitment phobe, remember that these people tend to fear commitment in multiple areas of their life and making plans is no exception. If you suggest dinner for a Friday on a Monday and you get shut down with an, "I don't know, maybe, we'll see, I might have plans," you'll know why. Another reason plans might wait until last minute is because the person in question doesn't want you getting any wrong ideas. Making plans ahead of time means that person is worthy of saving a time slot for. *And that's some serious shit.*

You're much too clingy

Another red flag, that may leave you incredibly confused, is being told you're taking things too seriously when in reality, you're only reciprocating what you *thought* the person in question felt for you. But to a commitment phobe, expressing any kind of interest in something more serious than a fling is a huge no-no. So when all else fails, they will say whatever it takes to get you to back off. Some will even blatantly hurt you to try to get you to leave. If you find yourself in an inexplicably confusing situation, it might be for a reason.

♥

The above warning signs are just a few. You may find one and you may find a combination. The most important thing is to not turn a blind eye just because you don't like the path something is taking. Deep within, like all other warning signs in this book, you know something is wrong. It's just easy to ignore it when you mix a little denial with a bit of wishful thinking.

The Types

Commitment issues are such a common topic in relationship conversations that this chapter has to be approached tactfully. Writing essays on the matter won't do anyone any good. Maybe that's why this chapter is action packed with lists. It's a clean mathematical equation, right? *Right.*

Now that we've got some background on the reasons why these issues exist and how they can manifest themselves, let's take a look at the person in question. Who, exactly, are you dealing with?

The Blunt One

Some people don't want to be in a relationship. Maybe it's a break they're taking; maybe they've just never wanted one. Regardless of the reason, this type has made it clear from the start that nothing serious is going to come out of your fling.

The Bullshitter

This type tells you exactly what you want, and often *need,* to hear in order to keep the fling alive without the commitment. You're probably hearing things like, "I want to change, I really want to deal with my issues and be with you." Yet you're not getting the commitment and it doesn't seem like any progress is being made. That's because the Bullshitter is having his cake and eating it too.

The Scaredy Cat

The Scaredy Cat is the only one with the real phobia. Maybe there's a broken home in his past or maybe an ex has forever wounded his faith in monogamy. Whatever the reason, this person is scared shitless of taking things to the next level and you're the one left empty handed.

Why are these labels so important? Because, labeling

it is your ticket to knowing what to do with it. As a friend, I'd tell you to walk away from the Bullshitter with the hit it and quit it track record that is just in for the thrill of the chase. I might, however, suggest you stick around a tad longer for the Scaredy Cat with the broken home. Nothing a little therapy can't fix, right?

In other words, it's not fair to attack someone who has made it clear that commitment was nonnegotiable. You need to take everything into account before trying to deal with someone that has issues with commitment. If you jump the gun without doing your homework, you not only risk looking like a desperate fool, but you also risk ruining something that might have had a chance. Speaking of which, *now what?*

Playing the Cards You've Been Dealt

You're almost ready to approach the object of your affection to make a case for monogamy. You've gotten all the information you need on what is going on behind enemy lines – but you're still a step short of success.

A relationship is between two people, even when the emphasis seems to only be on one. Sure, your new lover may have commitment issues that need to be addressed but whom do you think is going to feel their backlash? Who's going to end up with a broken heart if things don't go as planned? Who's left with high hopes and expectations, only to have them be continuously crushed? *You.* It's time you ask yourself some important questions.

- What are you in this for?
- What do you want?
- How important is monogamy to you?

- How about a label – i.e. boyfriend and girlfriend?
- Are you willing to share?
- Are you willing to wait?
- Is there anything you can do to help your lover through the phobia, if one even exists?

You're risking a lot by having feelings for a person like this – you need to be prepared. Knowing where you stand will make it a lot easier when, and if, you decide to speak up. Especially because there's a good chance you won't to be happy with the result. As previously mentioned, people who have issues with commitment are unlikely to do a 180 when cornered.

Another thing to keep in mind: a person with existing commitment issues is more likely to cause you pain – you know, in case you're successful in your attempts. Not only are they more likely to cheat, but they're also more likely to do things that hurt you, just to push you away. So what's the moral of the story? You're probably not the miracle cure he's been looking for. *You will not be the one to change him.*

Having said that, if the person in question has a genuine desire to deal with his or her issues, and you're willing to offer the support, there's a good chance it can work out. There are people out there with real fears that just need to know they have a support system around to get help. The desire has to genuinely be there, though. It can't be done with a 'reformed' player; he'll just cave to old habits. And when the 'reformed' player *is* ready to take on commitment, you'll never know he ever had a problem.

You're Worth More Than Having to 'Convince'

Assuming you're not dealing with someone with a diagnosed phobia, you should never find yourself in the position of having to 'convince' someone to be with you. I know, it sounds ridiculous when you see it on paper but you'd be surprised to know how many people are guilty of this. You can't help yourself. The feelings you have for that someone drive you, pull you and force you to act a fool. But does that make it okay?

In other words, get your head out of the clouds. You're putting all of your eggs into the wrong basket; a basket you bought from a discount store, marked down on clearance because it has a huge hole on the bottom. Sure, you can leave it up to fate and pray your eggs don't fall out but… who are you kidding? It's a risky thing to do. Spend the extra couple of bucks and buy one without the advertised hole. Catch my drift? *I'm not comparing love to purchases. If in doubt, read the paragraph again.*

You should be able to walk away. If it's a real commitment issue, your lover will deal with it and be at your door the second he's ready. Being available to someone without getting what you want in return will eventually bite you in the ass - regardless of how 'committed' you are to waiting. Misery will come knocking.

10. The One Sided Obsession

If you've ever had feelings for someone who didn't feel the same way about you, you know this can be a really painful experience. The one sided obsession can manifest itself in many different ways. You can want someone who doesn't feel the same, you can want someone who isn't yours to want, or you can want someone you once had but lost a hold of: your ex. Any way you slice it, you're obsessed with someone you can't have and it's about time you deal with your addiction. Let's take one variation at a time and dissect it, shall we?

Obsession # 1: Wanting someone who doesn't want you back

You finally gather the balls to approach your crush and get brutally rejected before you're even done poetically declaring your love. *Fucking fantastic.* (By the way, if you haven't spoken up, stop reading this book and call your crush. Although it puts you in a more vulnerable position, you'll never know if you aren't vocal about how you feel.)

So let's assume you declare your love and get rejected. First of all, know that it happens to everyone. It's part of life; maybe it's the universe's way of keeping things balanced, who knows. But it's important you *try* not to take it personally. People have types and you might not be the particular one that person has in mind. And you never know what that someone is going through in life – perhaps getting over a really rough break up? There are numerous reasons for rejecting someone and they don't all include your muffin top or your obsession with Star Trek.

Once you realize you've been rejected, it's time for you to take action; it's time to move the fuck on, not time to try and make a case for yourself. Many people attempt the PowerPoint presentation to showcase their worth. They think that if they try again, the person in question will suddenly realize they were wrong to reject them the first time around. If a physical approach fails, many people lie in bed and wish upon a falling star.

Reality Slap: Waiting for someone to want you back will consume you. Has it ever occurred to you that it may be beyond your control? Birthday wishes and drunken phone calls are fun and all, but they aren't going to bring your wishes to fruition. It doesn't mean you're ugly or not worthy of love. It just means this specific person doesn't want this specific relationship with you.

Obsession # 2: Wanting what you can't have

Another example of a one sided obsession is wanting someone who isn't yours to have. Let's talk about having feelings for your best friend's partner, for example. He should be completely off limits; he should be completely unattainable. But the moment he compliments you when you most need it, and you see how well he treats your best friend, he's your new prince charming. *What gives?*

What needs to be taken into account is the added element of desire that being unavailable brings to the table. Ask yourself if you'd still want that person if they weren't dating your best friend. Would you still constantly wonder how his lips would feel against yours? Would you still dream about the day he leaves everything behind to be with you? Maybe you have a jealousy induced personal vendetta against your friend – i.e. *She always gets what she wants!* When something is forbidden, it's suddenly the shiny, spanking new thing you've always wanted.

Your ego is at play. In a way, it's like asking yourself, "Wait, why can't I have him?" Once you devote a full night's rest to figuring out the answer, you'll conclude that the only thing standing in your way is your best friend. This is when your obsession begins. Eventually, the 'what could have been' mutates into a perfectly crafted fairytale you can't stop thinking about. You abandon all realities about the person – i.e. their inability to remain sober more than one night a week – and decide that the two of them will never last. The moment their relationship comes crumbling down, you'll be the one to benefit. *Dream on.*

Make no mistake: this doesn't *just* apply to wanting your best friend's lover. Wanting anything you can't have will send you straight into the land of delusional thinking. The moment you're left alone with your thoughts is the moment your obsession is feasting like a fat kid at Thanksgiving. You give it all the turkey it wants… and then it vomits all over you.

Reality Slap: There are two slaps needed for this delusion. The first slap resembles the one in the previous section: wishful thinking isn't going to bring your obsession to life. The second slap is to remind you that once you get what you want – if you get what you want – success will never taste as sweet as you have dreamed it to be. Without the added element of the forbidden, reality won't resemble the dream. Your time is better spent trying to figure out why you're attracted to the unattainable target to begin with.

Obsession #3: Wanting your ex back, bad

This section should have been it's own chapter. I'm keeping it short and sweet because a lot of it isn't anything you haven't heard before. This time I'm going to jam it so far down your throat that it's going to have to stick – your sanity depends on it. If all else fails, refer to the end of the book for added resources and make sure you read the corresponding chapter to address the situation with more attention to detail. (If you're trying to get over a cheater, for example, read Chapter 4)

Either you've been dumped or you had to do the dumping due to some unforgivable behavior. Regardless of how you got here, you can't get over your ex. Your ex, on the other hand, seems to be doing just fine without you. And while you've lost 10 lbs and are living off microwavable dinners, crying yourself to sleep every night, your ex is happily moving on in life. Let's face it: you're obsessed.

The question worth asking is simple: what are you waiting for? Break ups are hard to accept. It feels like one moment you're together, sharing the most intense love you've ever felt and the next you're ripping up photographs, wondering what the hell went wrong. Sometimes it's easier to assume it's just a glitch and that the two of you will be getting back together than having to face reality: you're over. And that's when *this* obsession begins.

Ex Scenario 1: Your shit of an ex broke your heart and you walked away... Didn't you?

You want nothing to do with your ex; whatever happened might be so unforgivable that the thought of being together again makes you sick to your stomach. So why, then, are you still up at night wondering what he or she is doing? No matter how hard you try, you'll daydream about the day your ex will come crawling back to you. You want to show off how much better you are now that the relationship is over. You want your ex to find out about your new lovers. It's all about you ex, blah blah blah... you're obsessed.

What's really going on: It's not about your ex; it's about your ego. The moment your heart was broken you knew, deep down, that you needed to end the relationship. But the fact your ex got to move on, after breaking *your* heart, hurts your feelings – and it's not fucking fair, either. You start to question the validity of the relationship the two of you shared. You want him to want you. *How dare he move on so quickly?* But how do you expect to move on if your every 'move-on' move involves your ex? Your daydreaming has nothing to do with how good of a person your cheating ex is. Take the time and work on your ego instead.

Ex Scenario 2: Your shit of an ex broke your heart and left you to rot

Your ex broke your heart, dumped you and you still want to be together. Wanting someone back who's treated you so poorly makes absolutely no sense, yet this is by far the most common of the 3 scenarios. You should have no problem moving on; knowing your ex hurt you so badly. So then why do you check your cell phone every minute of the day? Why do you turn the corner, hoping to find flowers on your doorstep? Why do you continue to call, email, text, and call again? You're handing your ex a beating stick and are obsessed with the pain.

What's really going on: It's your ego… again. You want your ex to realize he or she needs you and that hurting you was a mistake. You're also holding on to the good times, ignoring the bad and letting wishful thinking devour you whole. It starts by focusing on how much you loved each other when you were together. *Surely that kind of love has got to be one of a kind, right?* You didn't do *so much* for your ex, only to be told it was a dead-end, *did you?* Do you see the fairytale you're building by just asking yourself those two questions? Every time you masturbate to the way things were, you fall deeper and deeper into denial. You're willing to forgive the unforgivable and forget the unforgettable. Do the bruises you picked up along the way mean anything to you?

By holding on to an ex that caused you harm, you're subconsciously making yourself believe that's all you're worthy of.

Ex Scenario 3: You're the shit of an ex

You broke your ex's heart and are certain that a second chance would change everything, but your ex won't give it to you. You made a mistake and know he or she deserves more. But the thought of someone else being the one to supply it kills you. You're obsessed with making it right.

What's really going on: The reality that you may be a shitty person has just set in and whether or not you want to be with your ex again, you can't accept being capable of inflicting such pain on another individual. Here comes the ego again. If this is the first time you've screwed up, it's likely the feelings you have for your ex are driving your inability to let go of the relationship. If, however, you've been there and done that, you may want to ask yourself, *what's really going on here?* Are you trying to prove you're a good person to your ex...or to yourself?

♥

Reality Slap: There are definitely situations where a relationship needs time to breathe and then thrives once given a second chance. Unfortunately, chances are your scenario doesn't apply. Those times are rare. Things usually end for a reason and as hard as it is, you need to be prepared to look at things objectively.

Look at the facts. If he cheated on you, lied to you, beat you, or verbally abused you, why should you love him? What's admirable about a person who has broken your heart? What makes you stay up all night and wish things went back to being the way they were? Why are you obsessed with pain?

Failing to let go only prolongs the healing process. The day *will* come that you'll have to let go of this destructive delusion. And when you do, you'll have to endure hitting rock bottom to be able to climb back up to the top. Isn't it smart to save your strength for that long, hard climb rather than wasting it on something that's never going to happen?

The reason you're obsessing is because deep down inside you believe there's something you've missed. You stay up all night, analyzing every spoken word during the break up, wondering what could have been done differently. If you saw warning signs, you'll blame yourself for not fixing them right away and wonder why you hadn't. But the truth is simple: You will spend the rest of your life trying to find logic where there is none; love doesn't make *any* sense – to anyone. Over analyzing will not solve the puzzle.

Stop Obsessing

Let's face it: you're obsessed. It's pathetic and it needs to stop. We've already established the fact that obsessing doesn't help spring unicorns out of thin air. Enough excuses, enough hoping for 'what ifs' to come true, and enough wasting your life on wishful thinking; it's time to stop obsessing and become someone worthy of others' obsessions.

Don't let this obsession dictate your self-worth; unreciprocated emotions are like parasites to an individual's self-esteem. Remember that in the course of your life you're expected to go through a number of relationships. Fixating on the one with a person who shows no interest in you isn't going to do you any good. You should ex-pect most of your relationships to fail. If most relation-ships didn't fail, we would all end up marrying our high school sweethearts. *And how fucking boring would that be?*

The thoughts going through your mind while trying to get over a one sided obsession shouldn't be how to make that person want you. They should be all about getting over it and moving on with your life. If your head is clouded with unhealthy, obsessive thoughts, try the steps below. Whatever you do, just get over it!

Step 1:

Realize there are other reasons why he or she may not want to be with you.

- Getting over a break up
- Not looking to date
- They have a type and you're not it

It's not always a judgment on your personality or your looks. You may have a fantastic ass, but that does nothing for a boob man, catch my drift? There's nothing your obsessing can do to change the facts.

Step 2:

Take some time to compliment yourself; your self-esteem needs the hug. It doesn't have to be an arrogance parade but make sure to pat yourself on the back for that degree you've earned and for the six-pack you've worked so hard to achieve. Once you realize you're worth someone's interest, you'll get the confidence to move on.

Step 3:

Get the hell out there. How else do you expect to stop obsessing? *Out of sight, out of mind.* Get out there and feel the rush of meeting something new. If you keep moving on to the next possible suitor you're more likely to find one who feels the way you do. Unless, of course, you're into beating the shit out of yourself.

Obsessing over something will not make it come true. There are no love spells, no falling stars and no love devils to sell your soul to. By devoting your time to someone you can't have, you risk missing out on everything you *can* have. And believe me, when you reach the finish line you don't want to get there empty handed.

11. The Two Sided Obsession

In Chapter 10, we learned about you being obsessive. What happens when two people like you meet, think they fall in love and become *inseparable?* Consider how destructive one sided obsessions can be. Double the destruction and you've got yourself a big ass mess: a two sided obsession – **an unhealthy relationship between two people that is often mistaken as being passionate**. This is the last of the mirages because it's the hardest to get out of; because in these relationships, it's not just one person engulfed in a delusion, it's two.

You're constantly feeding each other bullshit to ensure you remain reliant on one another. It's a constant game of pushing and pulling, never letting each other go, no matter the circumstances. Without each other, you'd be completely lost – but not in a romantic way, more like in an obsessive dependent way.

This relationship is an extremely toxic drug neither of you can give up. First, we're going to isolate it. Then, we're going to attack the addiction and get rid of it for good. The first step is admitting you have a problem.

Obsessed With the Drama — Being Together

If you think this chapter is about your relationship, it probably is. You've become *that* couple: always fighting, quickly making up and repeating the same process immediately the next day. Your fights are intense, they're embarrassing and they take everything out of you, every time. Each tear you cry, you promise yourself you're done with the drama, yet you wake up needing each other like nothing had ever happened. You're obsessed with each other, and the vicious cycle that has become your relationship. *Sound familiar?*

Signs You're in a Two Sided Obsessive Relationship:

- *There is a constant flow of drama* – whatever the reason is you're fighting; you're always at each other's throats. You can never be in public without making a scene.
- *There's a lack of trust* – on both ends. You doubt one another's ability to be loyal. You feel entitled to snoop and invade each other's privacy. In your mind, you deserve to know your partner's whereabouts at all times.
- *There's always a threat to leave* – which only emphasizes how reliant you are on one another. It's almost as if to say, "You know you can't live without me, and I without you. Leaving will only kill us both. So please, don't make me leave… we both know it's not going to happen."
- *There's a lethal combo of verbal abuse and manipulation* – You weaken each other's confidence of surviving alone in the real world, again emphasizing how badly you need one another. It's a double dose

116

of Chapter 5, with the infliction of pain coming from every angle, creating a nook of painful isolation.

- *There's no one to console you* – Friends get so tired of hearing the same old crap and having their advice ignored that they often don't stick around to hear you bitch anymore. This leaves only one person to accept your crying with open arms: your partner – the guilty culprit. And that is the last person who should be consoling you.

When you fight, you never learn from either of your mistakes. What you may interpret as the two of you resolving your issues is really a façade. You don't deal with the root of the argument, you just brush it off and you use not being able to live without one another as an excuse.

It becomes your reality and before you know it, you're labeling the relationship deep and passionate when really, it's destructive and unhealthy. Think of it as a drug addiction. You get wrapped up in cocaine because it makes you think clearly and gives you the energy to finish the tasks on your to-do lists. Cocaine is your wonder drug, sort of like how your lover is your wonder-mate. What you choose to ignore is the fact you're dependent and can't get through the day without it. You ignore the amount of debt you've gone into in order to keep your drug around. Well, in an obsession-driven relationship it's the same ball game: you ignore the dependency and addiction and pretend it doesn't drain every fiber of your being. You're practically just inserting each other's syringes. *Cute.*

Can't Let Each Other Go — After a Break Up

We've covered the lingering period after a break up (Chapter 8) but what we're talking about in this section takes it to a whole new level. Lingering is inevitable; obsession isn't.

Unfortunately, even if one person finds the balls to call it quits, an obsessive relationship can often mutate into an obsessive break up: not letting one another move on. Going back to the drug analogy, this phenomenon could be compared to relapsing after a break through.

Even if one dumps the other, it takes two to completely break up and both parties are usually equally guilty when it comes to an obsessive break up. When one pursues, the other allows it; practically extending that tug o' war that was once the relationship.

Not letting go only prolongs the inevitable. Keeping one another on a tight leash only gives little bursts of pleasure, but ultimately, you're still headed for the same crash landing. When you're living with a broken heart all rationality goes out the window. You can't help but give into your emotions without worrying about the repercussions because, in your mind, shit's already hit the fan. *What's the harm?*

But remember: **You broke up for a reason.**

The tug o' war doesn't usually come from a genuine place, especially when the break up was long overdue. It usually begins with the confusion that comes with breaking up: you can't figure out exactly *why* things ended the way they did, especially knowing how 'passionate' your relationship had been to begin with. Then, once the confusion passes, you find yourself worried that your ex will move on before you do – and that just can't happen. See a pattern?

Not much of the 'holding on' comes from having genuine feelings for one another. You're doing what you have to in order to get your last hit, and so is your ex. This is going to go on forever if no one pulls the plug. What you're essentially doing is extending the relationship - without the title. So, tell me again: *what was the point of breaking up?*

The Obsessive Reality Slap

Being this addicted to one another does not mean that the relationship is meant to be; it does not mean it's passionate; and it definitely doesn't mean this is the only love you'll ever know.

The drama, the threats, the constant pushing and pulling... this is not what a healthy relationship looks like. In a healthy relationship, the two parties show support for one another and are able to communicate clearly, effectively and as selflessly as possible – because they genuinely love one another. In an unhealthy, obsessive relationship you're constantly building on the fear of losing one another. Healthy relationships promote individual growth; unhealthy relationships only promote themselves. It's easy to get the two mixed up when you're an addict.

During this game of tug o' war, one of you will eventually have to let go. Save yourself the calluses and be the one to do it first. The longer the game continues, the harder it'll be to heal the wounds and start your road towards recovery. You may shake your head and feel that comparing your relationship to a drug addiction is taking it a bit overboard but in reality, they're exactly the same. You know the consequences of doing cocaine, you simply choose to ignore them and pray they don't happen to you. It's the same when it comes to loving someone who is bad for your health. So it's time to let go.

12 Steps to Getting Over Your Addiction

The other person is sure as hell not going to end it; you're going to have to take matters into your own hands.

Step 1: Admit your relationship is unhealthy and that you have a problem

Remember when you were young, dreaming up your idea of the perfect relationship? Did it include harassing phone calls and jealous antics? Forget the person you're with. Is this the type of relationship you want to be involved with for the rest of your life? Is this the kind of person you want to be? You've got to admit that you're holding on to a fantasy that doesn't exist and that doing so is only hurting you.

Step 2: Realize a rope exists to pull you back to reality

We often settle for what we know as 'reality' because we couldn't imagine anything different ever existing.

That's what happens when you fall in love: you fall victim to a bad case of tunnel vision. It's important for you to realize that as easy as it was for you to create this reality, it'll be just as easy to destroy it.

Step 3: Find the instinct of survival buried deep within you

Once you've realized you've got a problem and that there's another world out there, the third step is finding the strength hidden deep within you to reach it. We are animals and the instinct to survive is there. It's just buried underneath all the superficial bullshit produced by our day-to-day lives. Why *wouldn't* being healthy, happy and truly loved be your ultimate goal?

Step 4: Surrender to the strength that is the instinct to survive

Once you find that strength, the hardest thing to do is to let go and embrace it. Let go of everything you've known, let go of the security this person provides, and let go of thinking this is all you're worth. Trust that instinct to lead you towards recovery and independence.

Step 5: Grab a piece of paper and confess everything you've turned a blind eye to

Chances are that at some point during your relationship/break up you've stopped to question the other person's behavior. If, for example, this person acted possessively and you shrugged it off as 'protective' that would go on this list. Admit everything you've never wanted to admit before, it'll help you see why distancing yourself and letting go is crucial in order to survive. This step might take a little longer than you'd like but it's important you devote every fiber of your being to being as honest as possible.

Step 6: Admit the role you've played in the obsessive relationship

It's a two-sided obsession. Intentionally or unintentionally, you've equally contributed to the tug o' war. Write down the ways you've contributed, interrogate yourself and try to figure out why you felt the need to behave that way. Is this a sign of something you're afraid to deal with in your past? Are you afraid of being alone? And above all else, is this the way you want to behave in future relationships?

Step 7: Forgive yourself

One of the most important steps in this process is being able to forgive yourself. You're not a clingy freak destined to obsess over every lover and relationship. Don't make yourself believe an unhealthy relationship is all you are worthy of. Forgiving yourself is a tough step because it entails an uncharted degree of honesty. Clump up steps 5 and 6 and get to the forgiving.

Step 8: Voice Step 5, 6 and 7 to the person

Things seem more real when spoken out loud. This step will be scary but it's crucial to accomplish. If the person in question is for whatever reason reluctant to listen, write it in a letter and send it. You will have done your part. It's also important to remember that the other person is equally as obsessed. At this stage you should be focusing on your progress while simultaneously muting out any resistance from the other end. Your ex will try to lure you back in. This is what makes it different than a drug addiction: your ex can talk, cocaine can't.

Step 9: Forgive the person for his/her part in the game

As hard as it may be, you've got to find a way to forgive the person for the role they played. If the damage seems irreparable, consider starting this process and making forgiveness the ultimate goal. What's important is to remember that as sure as everything seems as it's happening, life is unpredictable; people make mistakes and are often blinded by emotion – just like you've been in the past. Keeping forgiveness in your heart will help you move on.

Step 10: Commit to being honest with yourself, no matter what the reflection in the mirror shows

Coming to terms with our flaws is one of the hardest things to do. The last thing you want to admit is that you've played a role in the breaking of your own heart. Unfortunately, there is no progression if you don't hit rock bottom. Everyone has done things they aren't proud of – it's part of life. Don't run away from your reflection, no matter how ugly it gets.

Step 11: Learn from your mistakes, observe the 'healthy' around you and consider yourself a constant work in progress

As previously stated, we all make mistakes. What separates the winners from the losers is the ability to learn from those mistakes. Step 10 is a lot harder than this step, but this step has to constantly be active in order for it to work. Don't repeat history; learn from it.

Step 12: Don't contribute to other people's obsessive behaviour, instead reach out to them when you see it happening around you

Reaching out will help remind you of the struggle you went through. By the time you reach this step you should be able to see how bad things really were. In the midst of the chaos and the sugarcoated rainbow, it's easy to be fooled. But, when you see others going through the same thing it's always wise to reach out. Reach out once, offer the fact you can relate and then wait patiently. Think back to the blur of your two-sided obsession: could you have listened to someone who claimed to know what you were going through? Probably not, but would it have helped? *Absolutely.*

♥

It's a process. But if you don't deal with the root of your obsession, you're likely to fall back into it with someone else. There's a reason you are continuously seeking out the unhealthy and it's definitely not your lover's charming ways that keep you coming back.

You deserve to be happy, you deserve to be with someone who supports you and allows you to grow as an individual. Consequently, you should be in a place in your life where you're comfortably able to provide that for your partner, too. No relationship is the same, each has a shit ton of lessons to teach you, so be open to learning them.

Moving On

12. The Never-ending Story

We'd like to believe people are capable of change. Some are, but most aren't. And although 100% of you reading this chapter are certain you're dating the few exceptions that *are* capable of change, most of you are wrong. Are you willing to waste your life and every ounce of the energy within you to find out?

No matter what your relationship status is, it's easy to fall into this vicious cycle. The never-ending story applies to each mirage covered in this book. *How?*

1. Being the other person in an affair

Does any of the following sound familiar?

- Things are complicated right now
- He/she's going through a rough time
- I'm just waiting for the right time
- I just want to make sure *this* is real before I do anything drastic
- As soon as I'm ready, I'll tell him/her about you

How long are you willing to wait? There are people

out there, available people, willing to make you their number 1 choice and yet here you are listening to the same chorus on loop. Your lover will not leave his lover; no matter the bullshit he wants you to believe.

2. Being with a cheater

Sure, there's a chance the person you're with made a mistake and will never do it again, but truthfully, the chances are slim to none and you know it. The reason this mirage is likely to become a never-ending story is simple: even if you don't catch your partner between the sheets with someone else, chance are you'll always suspect it. And as tempting as living a paranoia-filled life may sound, it takes a lot of work from both parties to make infidelity a thing of the past.

3. Being with someone who verbally abuses you

The insults, secrets and manipulation come from something that goes a lot deeper than your relationship. You might be able to come to some sort of an understanding that provides short-term relief. But unless your partner seeks outside help, those issues are bound to resurface and you'll be the one to take the beating. Justifying abuse will come much too easily to you and walking away will become much harder.

4. Being with a bloodsucker — the leech

We are creatures of habit; it's hard for people to do a complete 180-degree turn if they're used to getting what they want. Unfortunately, chances are the feelings you share aren't enough of an incentive to get your leechy lover to change. When confronted, these people seem to do one of two things: they either work harder at their ability to drain you, or they start looking for another victim. Why stick around to feel the backlash of *either*?

5. Being with someone who physically abuses you

Much like the third mirage, abuse usually occurs when deeper issues are at work. To be put simply, your life is at stake. Even if your partner seeks *serious* help, this should be done without putting your safety at risk. It's important to know that because the abuse isn't about *you*, it's likely to continue and most of the time, it will.

6. Beating it into the ground

You're unable to let go, which is why you're still beating this failed relationship into the ground. This scenario is the epitome of a never-ending story. But know that there's a reason it's not coming back to life and that it's time to embrace reality.

7. Committing to someone who doesn't want to commit

If you're patient, there's a *possibility* the object of your attraction will *eventually* come around. But most likely, you'll just end up being the bang on the side, ready to spread 'em at the first sign of hope. Reformation takes time; if you're aware of existing commitment issues, there's a good chance it won't happen while you're around. Things will probably seem perfect to you and worth the wait, but beware, the situation is unlikely to change.

8. You're obsessed

Wishing on a falling star doesn't really work. It doesn't matter how hard you obsess over someone who doesn't want to be with you; the story will never change. The obsession is rooted inside of you and there is little you can do to make someone love you.

9. You're both obsessed

If someone doesn't put a stop to it, the game of tug o' war will go on forever. You will continue to feed each other bullshit until you're both so stuffed you regurgitate it back to one another. It's a disgusting addiction with a longer shelf life than a Twinkie.

♥

As you can see, I'm not making any of this shit up. If your situation had hope, it's very unlikely that you'd be reading my book. You're probably at the point that you need it shoved down your throat a few times for it to really sink in: nothing is going to change.

When you're together

There are a few reasons why things don't change: it's you, your partner, or the both of you combined. It's important you figure out the reason your relationship has become a skipping record. If you can't pinpoint the culprit, or take responsibility for your own actions, you'll be stuck in the loop forever. Do yourself a favor and take out the fucking disc.

Because of You

There's a fine line between being supportive and being a doormat. Have you crossed it? It's not a crime to give second chances and most of us have done so at one point in our lives. But when you allow the behavior to repeatedly continue, the person in question no longer worries about losing you. Even if you say, "Things need to change", your actions speak otherwise and the person goes on his or her merry way, having the cake and eating it too. If you're not okay with something, you have to take a stand and follow through.

Because of Your Partner

Unfortunately, some people are just shitty people with issues that extend much further than you could ever imagine. Your partner's behavior is, in a sense, independent of your actions with no plans to change. When you are ready to leave and give up, you're fed the exact amount of bullshit you need to hear in order to stay. That's not a coincidence either. For some reason, your partner loves his or her ability to keep that record skipping and you love listening to it.

Because of Both of You

When one is ready to make a change, the other person does everything in his/her power to keep them wrapped in the mirage; it's a never-ending cycle. When

The 9 Mirages of Love

both parties are to be blamed for the never-ending story, you're bound to encounter extremely unhealthy delusional thinking with no one able to deliver the necessary dose of reality. If someone doesn't stand up and walk away, this relationship *will* go on forever.

When you're not together

The mirage is all in your head. You and only you have the power to end it. In your mind there's no reason to stop it. Love can blind you and make you believe things you want to believe. The feeling of euphoria takes over, why would you want to give up such a high?

I'll tell you why: because it's not real. It's synthetic. It won't last; you'll devote your life to feeding a fire that provides no warmth. It's an illusion and you've got two choices: either you stop it or you dive into a dream world only making the fall towards reality harder to bear. Reality always catches up, do you want to be all drugged up when it does?

There's a reason these are called mirages. You're deluding yourself. Reality can often be pretty dry and uncomfortable to endure. It's easy to imagine a big pool of water surrounding you when you most crave it. But what satisfaction does it provide if it doesn't really exist?

Reality Slap: You're busy investing every fiber of your being to a damaged relationship – all in the name of love. You're ignoring the pain it's causing you and relying solely on the hope that your love is strong enough to make things change. While you let your life pass you by, you're chipping away at your chance to be happy. There are many people out there that won't let you down, but you'll never meet them because you can't tell it's time to move on.

I get it; it's hard to stop a skipping record if you don't have a new, working one to replace it, especially when you *love* listening to the same song. But how do you expect to find a new one if you never leave the house because you're hoping the old one will just start working again? Give yourself the opportunity to meet new people; people whose actions might just surprise you – unlike the predictability of the never-ending story.

13. A Guide to Breaking Up

As much as I love the sound of my fingers diligently typing away on this keyboard, this book was written with a purpose. And if you've gotten to this chapter, you should be ready to take the next step: breaking up. If you're looking to hear about rainbows, butterflies and everything else that love can achieve, you've picked up the wrong book. This isn't a book founded on pessimism; I'm here to tell you that you're worth more than chasing something that may or may not – but probably doesn't- exist. Having said that, I'll save the sappy shit for the next chapter. For now, let me help you get through the big, scary process of actually letting go.

Breaking Up: A Guide

Each step is crucial; without completing step 1, you may not advance to step 2. If you try to cheat and skip steps, you'll end up miserable, collapsing into a world of repetitive pain. Lying has gotten you into this mess; so make sure to be honest with yourself. Some steps take longer than others while some are easier to accomplish.

Regardless, each step has to be completed before moving on to the next or you'll render the entire process worthless.

Step 1: Realize the Relationship Has to End

After barely scratching the surface of how much damage this relationship has caused you, it's important you absorb everything you've learned thus far; there will be more to face with time, don't worry. Don't ask yourself whether or not your partner loves you, that'll only cloud your judgment. Instead, ask yourself whether you deserve to be cheated on; or beaten; or insulted; or led on, etc.

As 'negative' as this book may come out to sound, the truth is simple: this relationship is considered shit compared to the many non-shitty ones out there – you've just been blindfolded and put into a deep, dark cave. You may think letting go is the hardest thing to do and that you'll never find love like the kind you're experiencing now, but you're wrong.

This is why the first step is considered the very hardest to accomplish. You have to look into the mirror, strip down and be completely honest with yourself. Is the 'love' and 'security' you think you feel worth the pain you're experiencing? Because, after all, you *are* experiencing pain, aren't you? That's why you're reading this book. You don't deserve it and the previous chapter should have convinced you that nothing is going to change. So why are you committing yourself to a life of pain when there is *so much* more out there?

Exactly. Step one is realizing that, beyond all doubt, this unhealthy, relationship-mimicking mirage has got to end and you're going to have to be the one to do it.

Step 2: Make a Promise to Yourself

The problem with love is that it gives us the ability to lie to ourselves. We will rationalize every situation and justify every mistake, twice. There will come a time, if it hasn't already, that you won't know what to believe. You will have become so talented at fooling yourself into thinking certain behaviors are the norm, that your partner wants to change or that you deserve how you're being treated. The truth is, you don't. But who's going to tell you that, and how in the hell are you going to believe it?

This is why the relationship you have with yourself is *so* important. You have to be able to look in the mirror and shed it all – the good and the ugly. Beat yourself up, apologize for lying to yourself and strike a deal with your reflection: from now on, you're going to be completely and utterly honest with yourself, no matter what. If you see a wave of denial approaching, turn around – no matter how badly you want to give in. After all, step 1 did assure you this relationship has to end. Trust yourself to guide you towards 'salvation' because no one else is going to do it for you. Tell yourself you *are* worth it - every day if you have to.

Before you take any further action in the process, it's crucial that you complete this step in its entirety. You're going to need yourself on your side because if at any point of the game you decide to give in to the wishful, delusional thinking that created the mirage in the first place, you won't have anyone but yourself to help you out.

At this point, you know damn well this relationship has to end and that you're a lot stronger than you give yourself credit for. If you don't look out for your best interest, **no one else will.**

Step 3: Have the Talk

On the surface, this may seem like the hardest step to accomplish. Facing the storm is a scary, scary process. Imagine you are your own lawyer inside the courtroom and your entire career depends on you successfully defending your own case. Your case, in this situation, is your romantic wellbeing and your happiness; it deserves the best representation. Don't be scared, if anyone in the world knows what you deserve and what you want in life, it's you. *Own it.*

Breaking up is a big deal. You may be ending a three yearlong relationship; you may be ending a passionate affair that's only lasted a few months. You may just be breaking up with an obsession. Regardless, you're obviously in deep enough that you can no longer see clearly and that's why breaking up is such an intense process; it's not about the duration, it's about the emotional investment.

That is why it's important to do it face to face. In today's world, if you're a chicken shit, you can easily send an email. Even things we used to do over the phone have migrated to text messages. Electronic devices and social media give us a wall to hide behind. But what the hell are you so scared of? You are standing your ground and voicing what you deserve as a human being, right? *Right.*

Maybe you're scared of your partner's reaction. Maybe you're worried you'd cave if you saw the puppy dog eyes looking back at you once you've done the deed. Whatever the reason for your fear, shove it out the window. And don't try to give the old 'it's not worth it' excuse. No matter the crime, every relationship deserves the respect of being acknowledged face to face. Except, of course, if you're ending a physically abusive relationship. In such cases, you *most definitely* want to avoid a face-to-face encounter.

Take a deep breath before approaching your partner. You want to come off strong and confident yet non-combative, no matter the pain you're feeling inside. This is important for a few reasons. First of all, you need to be taken seriously – no one likes the boy who cried wolf. Secondly, it's important you're wishes are respected; otherwise anyone who feels they have the power to hurt you will believe they can easily override any of your demands. Thirdly, hearing yourself say the words out loud, with strength and confidence, will help you believe they're true.

You don't want to come off combative because, remember, you're not here to offer a second chance. You're here to tell your partner you no longer want this relationship. Watching you walk away is enough of a slap in the face; you don't need to revert to childlike name-calling. A film of the incident will continue to play in your head, over and over again; make sure it's something worth watching. Remember that the day will come when you will no longer feel resentment towards your past. **Act like the person you want others to see; make yourself proud**.

End 'the talk' by requesting the two of you have no contact. This includes texts, calls, emails, snail mail and voicemails. In fact, go ahead and un-friend your ex on Facebook and un-follow them on Twitter, while you're at it. These mediums are much too dangerous these days and can severely hinder your recovery.

If you face your fears now, the healing process will be a lot quicker.

Step 4: Keep Your Foot Down

As we mentioned before, complicated relationships have the tendency to linger. This is by far one of the most important steps in the process: keep your foot down. You did not accomplish steps one, two and three successfully only to fail and start all over again. You're over the hard stuff. This is where your journey to recovery *really* begins.

Having no contact is *vital* to successfully recovering from a break up. What's even more important is that you follow through with it. That means no late night drunk calls, no 'accidental' texts, no checking your ex's Facebook through your friend's account, etc. Being in touch will only confuse you, even if the two of you ended on a good note and are adamant about remaining friends. If the friendship is meant to be, it can wait.

If you don't keep your foot down and hold strong, it'll undermine everything you've achieved thus far. Your credibility is at stake; remember that no one respects the boy who cried wolf. And if you don't keep your foot down, what kind of message do you think that'll send your ex? It'll only reaffirm the things he/she was certain of, consciously or not, throughout your relationship: that you're weak and easily trampled.

You're not weak; you're strong. You've come *too* far to go back. You deserve better, better than a delusion. You're at the hardest part of the process; stand strong.

Step 5: Mourn in Private

No matter what your ex did to you, no matter what he/she made you believe and no matter how awesome you felt about the break up, you are bound to encounter moments of weakness. These moments range from the typical 'that used to be our favorite spot' to full blown nights of ice cream, stupid movies and hemorrhoid cream to de-puff the eyes. And if you're a guy, we're talking nights of black out binge drinking.

Words cannot describe how important it is to experience this part of the process. No matter how shitty the person you were with was, or is, there were obvious moments of joy, laughter and genuine love. It's important to acknowledge them in addition to the pain your ex caused you.

So it's extremely important to mourn the loss of your relationship, and it's even more important to do so privately. No one wants to read about your break up through Facebook updates and you don't need to announce your heartbroken state to the rest of the world in 140 characters or less. This, of course, excludes close friends; you need those. The 'privately' refers to avoiding public trash talking and pity parties. We've all had our hearts broken, and we've all got our own shit going on. Your cheating boyfriend doesn't warrant more attention than me losing my job, or being diagnosed with a terminal illness. *Catch my drift?*

In addition to respecting the privacy you deserve, there's another reason you should limit your public dear-diary moments: future possible suitors. No one wants to play doctor to someone else's broken heart. And if they do, they're not healthy relationship material. The more you radiate strength and composure, the more people will be drawn to you.

It's important you know this does not mean to put on a show for the rest of the world. Put a smile on your face but don't throw a party, get what I'm saying? If ending a long-term relationship is taking it's toll on you, be vocal about it and say nothing more. "I'm getting over a rough break up, but I'll be fine soon enough." That's honest and optimistic. Isn't that a little easier to hear than, "Fucking asshole fucked my best friend. Doesn't matter, he had a small cock anyway! I'm planning on fucking the entire basketball team! Anyway, what are you doing later?"

Step 6: Work on You

The day you see that ray of light shine through your window, which you will, you'll want to run outside and showcase your goods for the next contestant. But as tempting as rebounding may seem, you need to refrain.

You've accomplished so much and gotten so far but you're still at risk for relapse. Think about it: there must have been a reason you were attracted to something so bad for you, right? You need to figure out the answer before you dive into anything new and this step does not happen over night. *I know it's a shame because hottie next-door looks like a whole lot of fun.* But you're now in the re-bound zone. You're in the time frame where your sub-conscious still wants to self medicate and quick fix the trauma it has experienced in the recent past. You can't let it.

Ask yourself why it was so easy to fall into such de-nial. How did you end up in the desert, seeing pools of water surrounding you? If the answer you come up with doesn't involve you, try again. The shitty part of life is having to come to terms with our mistakes in order to learn from them. Unless, of course, you're hungry for another dysfunctional, heart-breaking relationship; in that case you're a lost cause.

The truth is you play a bigger role than you know.

Think back to your parents, is there anything in your past that might be affecting your decisions today? Is there anything about you, specifically, that might have drawn you to your partner? For example, you might have been drawn to a low life leech because you have the tendency to want to take care of others. Take that in, let it soak and work on it.

Take the time to work on whatever you come up with. As mentioned before, you don't have to share any of this with anyone. This is part of your evolution as an individual, so that you don't repeat your mistakes. Life is about self-improvement and the individual's journey. The goal is to make it to tomorrow just a little bit wiser.

Step 7: Start Dating Again!

There are two rules to following this last step: 1) Give yourself enough time between relationships and 2) Dive back in with the same childlike curiosity and hunger as you did your last. Both rules are equally important and should be taken seriously.

If something deep inside you is telling you that you're not ready to begin another relationship, listen. There is no right or wrong amount of time one should wait before giving love another go. Some breakups warrant a longer recovery period; others are easily dismissed. At this point, you're the only one who knows. This is another reason the previous steps are so important: you should trust yourself enough to know when you're ready. And hey, if you make a mistake, you'll know; it's okay to realize you just might need a little more time on your own.

What you don't want to do is jump in *before* you're ready. If you do so, you not only risk damaging the progress you've made but you also risk developing false expectations of others. Furthermore, you risk attempting to self-medicate. None of the above scenarios lead to a healthy relationship. Remember not to fear being alone.

Having said that, some people get irrationally traumatized from past relationships and will do everything in their power to avoid a repeat – even if it means becoming asexual hermits. Here's the thing: **your next lover is not your last lover**. That's what this entire process was about. By taking the time to analyze yourself and working on your own issues, you will have eradicated a good chunk of the chance of dating someone like your ex.

Life is about experience. You have to survive the bad in order to not only appreciate but also *see* the greatness in front of you. Each person brings a new dish to the table, a new lesson for you to learn, a new part of yourself to discover and a new experience for you to remember. You can't hold others accountable for the actions of one individual. If you do, you're signing up for a lifetime of solitude. Remember everything great about falling in love? Do you remember the racing heart, the butterflies in your stomach, and the never-ending texts? That is why we fall in love: for the rush.

Or you can always become an asexual hermit, leaving the house to go to work and come straight home... masturbating every chance you get. That works too.

It may seem like the end of the world to you right now, but I promise you it's not. You will get through this and you will come out shining brighter than ever before.

14. A Mantra

Remember when you were young and dreamed about love? If you're a girl, you probably started a check-list of qualities your prince charming was going to possess – i.e. blonde hair, blue eyes, reminiscent of Devon Sawa in the movie *Casper*. If you're a guy, you might have masturbated to the thought of one day being with a hot chick who let's you play video games all night without hassling you or demanding romance. Whatever your dream once was, don't you ever wonder how you ended up with the person you're with now? *What the fuck went wrong?*

Checklists and masturbation material never incorporated a broken heart. And while it's true that in adolescence love is a lot less complicated than it is in our adult lives, why have we been able to let go of our standards so easily? Since when do you not deserve your dreams coming true and what the hell makes you think this is your last shot at happiness? *Do you think your cheating; manipulative, abusive partner is the best out there?*

Somewhere along the line, we learned to forcefully make relationships work rather than waiting for one that works on it's own. That is not to say relationships are easy by nature; even the most perfect of couples have their hurdles to surpass. I'm talking about making the cheater puzzle piece fit or giving the guy who calls you a whore a second, third and fourth chance because you feel you have to in order to 'make it work'. *Why?*

Love is not a punishment. You do not deserve to be treated like shit and you do not deserve the shame and pain that come along with loving someone who treats you like it either. Love isn't supposed to send you to bed in tears every night, it's not supposed to drive you to constant irrational thinking and it sure as hell isn't supposed to make you feel that hole at the pit of your stomach; it's supposed to fill it.

While you're sitting at home obsessing over something as unstable as a nonexistent pool of water in a desert, you're missing out on life. Before you know it, you'll be married to someone who takes you for granted. You're worth more than that and you deserve happiness. You'll never encounter that happiness if you don't take a look in the mirror and realize that life is just passing you by.

There are so many people in this world, with stories to tell and lessons to teach, waiting to meet you, craving to be blessed by your presence. You deserve to feel wanted, loved and cherished. You deserve to be supported and challenged. There are people out there dying to be that for you. Stop wasting your time on this toxic obsession; let go of the hope that someday it'll all turn around.

Real love is supposed to be an invigorating feeling. It's supposed to send you to the rooftops, screaming your lungs out in ecstasy. It's supposed to paint the world pink and flood you with optimism. It's supposed to encourage you to grow, develop and blossom as an individual. It's supposed to make you feel invincible, ready to take on anything the universe sends your way.

You have to take the future into your own hands and create the life you want to live. If you don't, someone else will do it for you. And how in the hell do you expect them to know what was on the checklist oh so many years ago? How is anyone supposed to know what you masturbated to when you were 16?

There's a whole world out there. Go live it.

A note to my readers

ChiaraSays.com breathes and grows because of you. You tell me what you're going through and I write a piece to help you. Almost every new visitor that comes to my website comes because of you. You're the reason I've realized writing is what I love to do.

I'm not asking for you to drop your panties and stand on a corner to sell my book. But what I *am* asking for is your word of mouth support!

If you dig an article on the website, share it on Facebook. If you think this book will help a friend in need, pass it along! Reality slaps make *great* birthday gifts.

I am busting my ass doing all of this on my own. I manage my own website, write my own articles, and self publish my own books. I rely on your voice to help me through it!

So follow me on twitter! Join me on Facebook! And always feel free to email me if you need any advice. Depending on my inbox my responses are pretty prompt and detailed. If you've got ideas for the website, send them my way. ChiaraSays.com is intended to reflect issues everyone deals with on a daily basis; the possibilities are endless.

I love you,
Chiara

Appendix A: You're Being Led On

You meet and things seem great; you could see yourself falling. Yet despite the attraction you feel, they're not ready and want to take it slow. Sound familiar? Taking things slow is fine with you until you catch yourself questioning whether or not they're even really interested in you. And so begins the painful realization that you're being led on.

Signs You're Being Led On

- You're always the one who makes the effort to hang out, hardly ever the other way around
- You never get the first text unless they're asking something of you
- When you do get a text or an effort it's usually a lonely one -i.e. late enough for other plans to fall through or just a need to 'cuddle'
- If you make a move, it's too fast and if they do it, it's just the right time; they call the shots on the pace of your relationship
- Their behavior confuses you and when you ask them about it, they get defensive
- You notice the insane amount of excuses you're always being fed
- The second you show a little lack of interest, you're instantly fed a bit of rope to keep you

wrapped up tight
- You notice you're always at their beck-n'-call

Although there are other 'dead' giveaways that you're being led on, these are the MAIN things to watch out for. If they're not enough to convince you, ask your close friends… they'll definitely have some extra input on the matter.

Why he/she is leading you on

Once you realize you're being used as a doormat, the next natural thought to pass through your mind is: but why? There are many reasons people get off on wrapping others around their fingers, below are just a few:

- You could be the stand-in until someone better comes along- no one likes to be lonely
- They could genuinely NOT be ready, in which case they've got no business 'dating' around, anyway
- They need the ego boost; nothing more invigorating than having someone at your disposal
- You're providing them with something they need -i.e. room and board, ride to work, an orgasm, emotional support, money, etc.

Moving On and Letting Go

Unless you get off on being a doormat or a psycho over analyzing the minutest details, it's probably in your best interest to move the hell on from this situation. But how the hell are you supposed to do that? You're hooked!

Approach:

To rid yourself of any doubt, approach the object of your affection and make your feelings known. Let them know how you feel and what it is you want, ideally, out of this 'relationship'. Be careful not to make it sound like an ultimatum; instead, defend your approach as an explanation for your behavior. If you still get fed bullshit, be it the same or something new, at least you won't have to defend your walking away.

Sometimes it helps to isolate what it is you really wanted in the first place. If, for example, you realize being together was your ultimate goal, them not being ready for a relationship kind of screws with your plans, does it not? People can have a genuine attraction but if the timing is wrong, giving it a premature shot could lead to disaster.

Note: This does NOT mean wait around until they're 'ready'

After being patient and attentive and professing your love, you've really done everything you could. You can't force someone into something they're a) not ready for or b) don't want. Give the person a day or two to think it over and then let the healing process begin.

You're the catch. The second you value yourself as that someone only worthy of being a 'pending application', you become it. While you're waiting for someone who may or may not be sleeping with everyone but you, you're missing out on meeting someone worthy of your love. Why invest in something that just keeps stealing your money and never giving anything back in return?

You'll do everything in your power to justify this person's behavior because the idea of them not being ready for a commitment sounds a lot better than them not wanting to be with you. And although there's always a slight chance they're telling the truth, 9 times out of 10, they're not.

Appendix B: Closure – Moving the Hell On

A pretty common complaint you'll hear from a broken hearted friend is the fact he or she – usually she – needs 'closure' in order to move on. Fine, that's fair. There are a few things you need to do in order to get that closure. First and foremost, stop fucking (no brainer, right?) Make sure you analyze your request, and finally, face reality and prepare yourself for a nice, hard slap. Intrigued? Let's go on…

Step 1: Stop Fucking

A one time shag after a break up is almost mandatory in this day in age; it doesn't always end on a good note but it often helps you realize that the relationship is over. Continuous, self deprecating contact, however, does absolutely no good for either party and only prolongs the inevitable – making it even harder to accept.

You don't physically have to be 'fucking' for this Step 1 to apply. You could be emotionally fucking too. This includes anything that makes you believe there is hope left, floating somewhere in the universe. Give it up because you're just deluding yourself.

In other words – don't expect to get any sort of closure if your genitals are still attached – physically OR emotionally.

Step 2: Analyse Your Request

What is it you *think* you need in order to move on? What *exactly* is left 'undone' that needs to be 'stitched up'? Do you *really* need to know why your ex broke your heart? Sometimes, you do. But other times, knowing that someone broke your heart should be enough reason to turn around, walk away and never look back.

When you're going through a break up, you have the ability to make yourself believe anything you want. If you just want to know the details of an affair out of curiosity, you can easily tell yourself you need to know them in order to move on. You don't realize you're just inserting the knife deeper and deeper by doing so.

Step 3: Face Reality

A chat on *why* he slept with your best friend isn't going to mend your broken heart. In a time of desperation, you'll look for any remedy to stop the pain. We've all been there. And sometimes, you'll need that extra slap in the face to realize it's time to move on – especially if you're still 'hoping' for something to happen. Regardless of what you feel you need to do, remember one thing: *The things you NEED to hear will never be what you WANT to hear.* That's usually what closure is… a very painful reality slap that leaves you walking away, saying to yourself, "Oh wait, *now* I get it…"

Guess what? You need closure to move on. But the closure you *really need* is attained within yourself. Being able to step outside the relationship and realize you're not meant to be and that it's time to let go is the ultimate path to salvation. Regardless of the choices you make – i.e. asking your ex why she fucked your football team – you will inevitably arrive at the point where you, yourself, realize it's time to walk away.

The day will come when you'll be over it. The question is what path do you plan to follow to get there? The relationship ended for a reason, the moment you find that reason is the moment you'll get your closure.

Appendix C: The Psycho Girlfriend – 8 Signs She's In Your Bed

You look at her over a candle lit dinner and wonder how you could ever be so lucky. She's everything you've ever asked for and everything you've ever masturbated to; she's perfect. But once the mask deteriorates, you suddenly find yourself in bed with a monster. Not sure? See if she meets the criteria:

8 Signs Your Girlfriend is Psycho

1. **Does she call, text, email, tweet or Facebook you constantly throughout the day?** If you're not actively participating, run. Whether she genuinely believes you never received her other texts or she just wants to make sure she stays on your mind, this is a BRIGHT red flag.

2. **How does she get her way in your relationship?** Does she sanely communicate her emotions or

does she use psycho tactics such as threats and misplaced tears? Beware of a woman who tells you she'll withhold sex if you don't do as she says. Other more common threats include, "If you go out with your friends, I'm going tell everyone your dick shrivels to a sad face when it's cold." And does she cry at the most inappropriate times? She can't ALWAYS be hormonal... can she?

3. **Does her alter ego erupt when she drinks?** Suddenly feel like you're dating Glenn Close in Fatal Attraction? Such behavior indicates a collection of deeply rooted issues and unless you're charging by the hour, this isn't the kind of baby-sitting you should be doing. Booze should never bring out the crazy in a person, and if it does, you need to get the hell out.

4. **Is she overly jealous?** Does she flip a shit at your kindness towards a female waitress? If you're constantly going out of your way to avoid contact with other women because you fear it'll be misinterpreted as a love affair, run. Remember that a good chunk of the population consists of women.

5. **Does she take steps forward in the relationship without you?** How big is her drawer at your place, REALLY? If you find yourself suddenly engaged without having purchased a ring, it may be time to reassess the situation. The psycho girlfriend has a funny way of making things happen without your consent. Don't let her trick you...*remain alert.*

6. **Are boys' nights out of the question?** Does she allow you to have a life outside of your relationship? If your girlfriend genuinely believes you should be attached at the hip at all times, the red flag has been waved. Is she

out of town? If so, she'll probably demand a play by play of each night's activities... and although secrets are not healthy, neither is having to give a headcount, name and background of every person present at a party. Oh, and beware of ANY woman who demands you "end it" with close friends and family members.

7. **Is she constantly snooping?** Whether it'd be cell phones, emails, Facebook, or your panty drawer, this is definitely scary behavior. It's almost as if she's saying, "If you don't INVITE me, I'll come in *ANYWAY!*" If the boundaries had been marked and she feels no need to respect them, you're definitely dealing with a psycho.

8. **Do you suddenly have a female doppelganger?** Suspicious that such a woman doesn't exist? You're probably right. If you find your girlfriend copying your every move and suddenly expressing interest in your most obscure hobbies, she's trying to ensure acceptance. And let's face it; the woman with a brand new buzz cut and obsession with Miller Lite is not the same woman you asked out to dinner.

All previous jokes aside, the psycho girlfriend is no laughing matter. Red flags such as the cling factor and methods of manipulation should **NOT** be ignored. A healthy relationship consists of two people who trust one another and are comfortable expressing fears and other emotions are they come. If you're still in doubt, even after the list above, ask your friends for their opinion- assuming they have yet to offer it.

If you're the psycho girlfriend, do you see how ridiculous you look? Stop now, seek help and regain the little dignity you have left. You're **NOT** ready to be in a relationship and you've got issues to be dealt with before you hurt anyone else. Stop embarrassing our gender and stop tempting every single male out there to carry a knife for protection. Not all women are crazy and we're sick and tired of you giving us a bad name.

Appendix D: 10 Signs You're Dating Mr. Possessive

Deep down inside, you know you don't need a 'Top 10 Signs' list to realize you're in an unhealthy relationship. The signs are there, you just need to identify them. If you're constantly making excuses for your relationship to friends and family, you know damn well something isn't right. You're probably shaking your head, thinking this couldn't happen to you… but you're wrong; it's a lot more common than you think.

Possessive relationships can start out mimicking the beginning of a healthy, insanely passionate relationship. But if you're not careful to make that distinction early in the game, you'll find yourself caught in a complete cluster-fuck.

And the problem is, it doesn't have to start off so intensely. You might have met Prince Charming, and then suddenly found yourself Sleeping with the Enemy. Realistically speaking, many of us would run at the first sign if it happened early enough – before becoming emotionally attached.

It's a lot easier to end up in one of these if-I-can't-have-you-no-one-can relationships. Here are a few red flags to keep your eyes open for:

10 Signs He's Possessive

1. He's constantly texting/calling you obsessively, even when you tell him you'll be busy for the day
2. Gives you shit for not responding promptly and accuses you of the craziest things
3. He won't allow you to be anywhere other guys will be. If you tell him it's an all girl thing, he'll check.
4. Needs constant updates and full recap of your previous night's activities: headcount, gender, venues, etc. Even as detailed as who you sat next to at the dinner table.
5. Your outfit needs to be approved before you step foot outside the door. Any area of skin that can give the wrong idea needs to be covered, or you're asking for it.
6. You're apparently fucking everything with a penis – even the postman.
7. He asks if you've fucked everything with a penis from your past and even when you tell him no, he'll hear yes.
8. He tries to isolate you from friends and family (because they're the most likely to tell you he's a nutcase)
9. You're expected to do as he says and will be punished if you don't. There is no such thing as compromise.
10. He gets defensive if anyone compliments you and thinks they're out to fuck you, whether there's a penis involved or not, you're no longer allowed to talk. Wouldn't want them Lesbos working their voodoo magic on you, would we?

I didn't include violence because that's a whole other article. But it's important to remember that guys like this are more likely to raise their hand to you.

Getting Out

A healthy relationship doesn't put you in a cage. When the two of you don't see eye to eye, you talk it out and compromise. You don't sign your life away when committing to a relationship; if that were the case, we'd all aim to be single forever. Recognize the signs above and get the hell out.

You'll be tempted to stay. He'll do everything in his power to manipulate you into giving it another change; he'll promise he'll change, he'll tell you he needs you and he'll tell you exactly what he thinks you need to hear. He'll temporarily turn into the model boyfriend, and you'll resume your stay at the insane asylum.

But I'm here to tell you, all of that is crap. Things won't change, they'll only get worse. And you'll be punished for having attempted to run; the chains will be one notch tighter. Don't be fooled: possessive tendencies are indicators of issues that need to be dealt with. Don't wait around to find out what those are.

Made in the USA
Lexington, KY
27 December 2011